"One cannot think
well, love well,
sleep well,
if one has not
dined well."

—Virginia Woolf,
A Room of One's Own

↑ Sadaharu Aoki

Photography by
Christian Sarramon

The Paris Gourmet

Trish Deseine

RESTAURANTS

SHOPS

RECIPES

TIPS

Flammarion

↑ Restaurant Jean-François Piège

On the menu

Introduction

" Trish Deseine is a veritable – and generous – gourmet. With her politically incorrect attitude towards sugar, cream and butter, she has shaken up home cooking, and made it accessible to everyone. She brings an Anglo-Saxon touch to cuisine that demystifies it and makes everything seem possible. What I love about Trish is that she makes cakes that taste great, that overflow with generosity and flavour, rather than making 'sensible' cakes – a girl after my own heart! "

– Pierre Hermé

Welcome to my little book of luxury, my ultimate pleasure, combining the city I love most with the subject I love most – food.

Just a few years ago, admitting such love, confessing adoration of something considered rather mundane (or hinting at a more than healthy appetite, especially for a woman), would have raised eyebrows. And when I was writing my first cookbook for French home cooks back in 1999, I remember one of my skinnier Parisian girlfriends, between puffs of her cigarette, asking me, rather disdainfully, 'Trish, don't you get bored thinking about food and cooking – all day?' Well, I didn't then, and I don't now. What's more, I'm not alone! These days, everyone's doing it, everyone has an opinion, and anyone can join in; food has become a reflection and an expression of so much in our lives – fashion, politics, art, history, philosophy, our emotions.

Paris has always offered itself up as the perfect playground for exploring all these avenues: you can eat in opulent temples of haute cuisine; *cafés littéraires*, resonating with history; hearty bistros; modern, world trend-leading restaurants; or romantic bars and cafés. Indoor and outdoor markets and the best food and artisan shops in the world are endless sources of knowledge, inspiration – and ingredients, for cooking at home.

I've been here for over twenty-five years, living in and around the city. First on rue de la Pompe in the 16th – an excellent, '*BCBG*' introduction to *les bonnes choses* of the Parisian food year. Then in the 15th, right over the rue Saint-Charles market, at which I rarely got to shop – too busy dashing to the metro to get to work as it opened, coming home long after it had ended. (I did become very friendly with my butcher, to the point of him obtaining real suet for me to make my Christmas pudding.)

↑ Popelini

For many years, when my children were small, I lived in the excessively food-loving town, just outside Paris, of Saint-Germain-en-Laye. Then I found the apartment of my dreams, a sixth-floor walk-up loft in the 19th, where the little triangle formed by the streets between the metros Jourdain and Pyrénées was a gourmet, yet *populaire* heaven. For a year or so I lived with my children in the very sedate 7th, with La Grande Épicerie de Paris as my local supermarket and the bistros and brasseries of Montparnasse our regular restaurants. And recently, my good luck found me a frugal, yet impossibly romantic studio on place des Vosges, and plunged me deep into the heart of le Marais, perhaps the part of Paris that most dreams of the city are made of.

Throughout these years I have loved, plotted, tasted, celebrated and commiserated at so many Parisian tables. I've watched food fashions come and go, and marvelled at how traditions live on and are so fiercely defended by the French. I have had three-star epiphanies, experienced Hermé macaron nirvana, survived Perigord truffle taste explosions, and cooked and cooked and cooked so much incredible produce.

↑ Marché Saxe Breteuil

La Tête dans les Olives →

↑ Au Bistro

And so, do I now feel like a Parisienne? Almost, but not
quite. I think my heart is, and will forever stay, Irish.
But I do feel that Paris, which can be so distant and aloof to
outsiders, has let me in a little and, in doing so, has become
completely necessary to me. I cannot go for long without
it – without its people, its food, its culture and its beauty.

Now, in these pages, I want to share a little of my Paris,
of all these gourmand, delicious years, with you. Give you
clues and pointers (and addresses!) to crack its codes.

Mostly I'm hoping, if you love food the way I do,
that this book will help you make the very most of the
world's most beautiful, most exciting foodie city as you eat
your way around it.

Baisers gourmands,

Trish

↑ La Pâtisserie des Rêves

i

My favourite addresses*

↑ 6 Paul Bert

**The restaurants
and shops that
keep me coming
back.**

These are the places that never let me down.
I selected them more for the way they can
influence my mood than for the food alone.
Nine times out of ten, I'll just want to sit with
friends in an authentic Parisian bistro. Now
and then, I'll feel the need to check out a new
hot spot and see what all the fuss is about.
Occasionally, I want to splurge on an elegant
venue that is one of the darlings of the
Parisian food scene. But a restaurant that
allows the conversation to flow easily gets
my vote over a purely gastronomic
'experience'. So while these places may not
all be hot or trendy, they have served as the
stage throughout the delicious story that
began when I arrived in Paris twenty-five
years ago. And now I'm giving them to you.
Please look after them.

Restaurants and bistros

Passage 53

A welcome retreat from the bustle of passage des Panoramas, one of Paris's busiest and prettiest covered arcades, invaded both by tourists and by suits from la Bourse nearby. The menus are set, leading you dreamily through small plates of great finesse and beauty cooked by the young Japanese chef, Shinichi Sato. Arriving at the restaurant just three years ago, Sato rapidly won two Michelin stars, the first Japanese chef in France to do so. His mix of French and Japanese techniques and produce is seamless. Rarely have I experienced a tasting menu where surprises and quantities are so balanced and gentle on both palate and stomach. The presentation is exquisite, Sato's creativity astonishing.

53, passage des Panoramas · Paris 2ᵉ · Tel. +33 (0)1 42 33 04 35
www.passage53.com

Le Timbre

The chef is English, the room tiny, with two rows of elbow-to-elbow tables
(only twenty-four places), and the menu succinct. But this is a charming
neighbourhood bistro with a cosy atmosphere and a nice touch on the
plate. Expect French classics with a little zing to keep them interesting.
A good place to bring the in-laws.

3, rue Sainte-Beuve · Paris 6ᵉ · Tel. +33 (0)1 45 49 10 40
www.restaurantletimbre.com

Le Baratin

Apologies for including the
obvious – this is many people's
favourite Parisian bistro. In my
defence, I did live just around the
corner for a few years so was
already using it pretty much as
a 'local' for early lunches and
late nights before the world's
critics started flocking after the
New York Times profiled Raquel.
As I write, the bistro has had
a bit of a facelift, with a spruced-
up façade, a lick of paint, new
seating – and Raquel is getting
to grips with her new piano.

Gentle and
enveloping.
Where feel-good
food lives.

3, rue Jouye Rouve · Paris 20ᵉ
Tel. +33 (0)1 43 49 39 70

Kitchen Galerie Bis

Fresh, light, super creative and subtly surprising.

The more relaxed little brother of William Ledeuil's famous Kitchen Galerie (hence the 'Bis' spinoff moniker), this is the first restaurant to make sense of the confusion of fusion. William is completely self-taught, getting to grips with Thai cuisine from books and available products before opening the restaurant and, subsequently, travelling to Thailand. Many years and many Asian travels later, William's technique, understanding and creativity had grown so much that Michelin awarded him a star for la Galerie. But I prefer this address. I love their marmites, deep aromatic dishes reminiscent of pho, marrying French lamb with a Thai jus, guinea fowl, chorizo and miso, cod, lemon, wasabi and shizo.

25, rue des Grands Augustins · Paris 6ᵉ
Tel. +33 (0)1 46 33 00 85
www.kitchengaleriebis.com

Restaurant
Michel Rostang

Old-school French, two Michelin stars, wood panelling, deep carpets, private rooms, (expensive) modern art and classical silver service *en salle*, so perhaps not everyone's cup of tea every weekend but thank heavens it exists. Snails, frogs' legs, foie gras, lièvre à la royale, canette au sang – it is somehow comforting to know that somewhere in Paris these dishes are still being served at this level of excellence in such a joyous atmosphere. Michel Rostang is one of the last guardians of *le repas gastronomique français*, and a man who knows how to handle truffles.

20, rue Rennequin · Paris 17ᵉ · Tel. +33 (0)1 47 63 40 77
www.michelrostang.com

Kitchen Galerie Bis ↑

Le Bis

This very pretty bistro used to be the annexe to the legendary temple of meat Le Severo (see p. 87). Now it's completely independent yet has maintained its carnivorous reputation in the neighbourhood with much talent. The oxtail and beef cheek terrine is chunky and tender and, a vital detail, popped under the grill for a minute or so as it comes out of the fridge before serving, avoiding the unpleasant gelatinous texture that can so often spoil this dish. The side salad's leaves were all reared in Annie Bertin's garden, and meet their end bathed in a perfectly seasoned vinaigrette – another detail often too rare in more luxurious surroundings. The heirloom tomato and burrata salad is deliciously fat and colourful; the desserts in keeping with the rest. A sure thing. Adorable service.

16, rue des Plantes · Paris 14ᵉ · Tel. +33 (0)1 40 44 73 09
www.restaurantlebis.fr

I love the
nooks and
crannies, folds
and corridors,
bars and
terrace.

Hôtel Costes

Critics have been known to carp at the modish predictability and the unimaginative presentation of the dishes here. But that is precisely why I love it. For the plainness hides a scrupulous attention to quality and detail by Jean Louis Costes *himself*. This is menu design at its best, where the food fits with the desires of the clientele like skinny jeans on Kate Moss. (She met Johnny Depp here – many moons ago.) The green beans are always perfectly crunchy, the spiciness of the dishes is carefully tuned and the sauces are served on the side to please both the fat cats and the supermodels that flock here during Fashion Week.

239, rue Saint-Honoré · Paris 1ᵉʳ
Tel. +33 (0)1 42 44 50 00
www.hotelcostes.com

For bon vivants – and Toby Jug enthusiasts.

Le Bistrot d'à Côté

Flaubert

The '*à côté*' (next door) is a reference to Michel Rostang's main restaurant, as the Flaubert is just one of Rostang's Parisian locations. The décor is warmly antiquey and the menu made up of many touches from Savoie, Lyon and Provence, all favourite regions of Michel's. Not the cheapest of neighbourhood restaurants, but *une valeur sûre*.

10, rue Gustave Flaubert · Paris 17ᵉ · Tel. +33 (0)1 42 67 05 81
www.bistrotflaubert.com

Au Bistro

This is in such an appealing street. I love that, just a few steps from worldwide style mecca Colette, you can find a butcher, a fruit seller and a few great little wine bars where local office workers are still the most faithful clientele. Au Bistro is similarly unsophisticated, with a rather strange, high banquette you have to climb into and tables which squash you into your neighbour's plate. Not a place to come with gossip or secrets. The food is hearty and very reasonable, given its location. It's a good place for French standards of snails, foie gras, oeufs meurette and steak frites. The service is brisk yet friendly enough, and it's OK to knot your napkin around your neck if you're worried things might get a little messy.

8, rue du Marché Saint-Honoré · Paris 1ᵉʳ · Tel. +33 (0)1 42 61 02 45

Lunch here if you skipped breakfast or are worn out from shopping.

Kei

I'm not a huge fan of set menus. Not that I mind being surprised or letting the chef express himself; it's just that whiff of convenience for the kitchen, of tired signature dishes mechanically rolled out. But at Kei, the *formules* will carry you along lightly and jubilantly, with 'Japanified' classic French cooking from Paris's Petit Prince, Japanese chef Kei Kobayashi. The dishes (four or five at lunchtime, more in the evening) are a series of refined little tableaux, never sacrificing taste for beauty and with gasp-worthy technical prowess (the milk chocolate mousse is at once hot and cold). It's a pretty formal, plush room, full of suits at lunchtime, but sometimes I love to do things properly. One of those reliable restaurants that feels like it's here to stay, in a city where, so often, young talent pops up and pops off.

Talent alert! Perhaps the most exciting cooking in Paris!

5, rue Coq Héron · Paris 1ᵉʳ
Tel. +33 (0)1 42 33 14 74
www.restaurant-kei.fr

Restaurant Chaumette

The very residential 16th isn't known for its restaurants and this is a neighbourhood bistro slightly off the beaten track. Opened in the 1930s by Mme Chaumette, set deeply off the street, with a few tables *en terrasse* snuggled under a low awning, this is a cosy spot for a comforting winter meal. At lunchtime it's full of journalists and actors from the nearby Maison de la Radio; in the evening, it's more grey-haired couples in cashmere and brogues. This is a good place to revise your French classics of blanquette de veau, chou farci, crêpes suzettes and millefeuille à la vanille. Don't miss the excellent onglet aux oignons when it makes the *carte du jour*.

7, rue Gros · Paris 16ᵉ · Tel. +33 (0)1 42 88 29 27 · www.restaurant-chaumette.com

Le Bistrot Paul Bert

Is this the perfect Parisian bistro? I think it could be. The space is pretty much all you could ask of a fantasy come true. Wooden panels, prettily tiled floors, mirrors and a chalkboard menu you could read all day until your rumbling stomach reminds you why you're there. The main room, with its bar and glass façade, is lovely for a long, people-watching Friday (*de préférence*) lunch. But in the evening you might prefer the cosier areas and banquettes in the far corner. Along with Benoît, the Paul Bert is my favourite place for serious black truffles when the season is in full swing and for generous 'proper' classic French desserts. Eggs with truffles, a vintage champagne, a Paris-Brest. Heaven for sinners.

18, rue Paul Bert · Paris 11ᵉ · Tel. +33 (0)1 43 72 24 01

This is where you'll find the DNA of French bistros.

6 Paul Bert

After the institution that is Le Bistrot Paul Bert and its little fish and shellfish brother, l'Ecailler du Bistrot, Bertrand Auboyneau continues his slow takeover of one of Paris's already most delicious streets with 6 Paul Bert, at number 6. He effortlessly brings the sublimely *franchouillard* bistro up to date with this long room, an open kitchen at one end and a deli at the other selling, amongst many *delices*, the most amazing jambon de Truie alongside Bordier butters and cheeses. The fabulous value of the original Paul Bert bistro menus (especially at lunchtime) is maintained, but here the cooking has been spruced up and lightened to a more modern state, with tasting plates and community tables – rapidly becoming *de rigueur* from Brooklyn to Shoreditch – bringing in a younger crowd.

6, rue Paul Bert · Paris 11ᵉ
Tel. +33 (0)1 43 79 14 32

Le Bistrot Paul Bert ↑

Le Châteaubriand

Another screamingly obvious member of my favourites club, but Le Châteaubriand is inextricably entwined with some of my most delicious moments of the past decade. Inaki Aizpitarte was Paris's first truly rock and roll chef, with zero pretence and incredible talent. He has managed to stay true to the values behind his cooking, keeping a tight ship amongst the Le Châteaubriand and Le Dauphin teams, while making a name for himself and subsequently influencing gastronomic experiences worldwide. I love that you can still have an off night at Le Châteaubriand when they fiddle with the tasting menu of the day and maybe go too far, and that they have not made things easier for themselves with signature dishes and the rolling out of concepts.

129, avenue Parmentier · Paris 11ᵉ · Tel. +33 (0)1 43 57 45 95
www.lechateaubriand.net

Inaki
Aizpitarte
dared.
Everyone else
followed.

Akrame

The room feels a bit stiff, a bit 1980s bland, but Akrame Benallal's spontaneous, buzzy cooking, which he learnt in Adria's and Gagnaire's kitchens, is always a tonic for a working lunch in a 16th arrondissement very lacking in *petites addresses sympas*.

19, rue Lauriston · Paris 16ᵉ · Tel. +33 (0)1 40 67 11 16 · www.akrame.com

Au Pied de Fouet

Possibly a dubious choice, given its tourist trap notoriety. But this was more or less my 'local' when I lived in the 7th and I grew to love the grumpy, crowded camaraderie of the place. It is still a very cheap, cosier version of, say, Chartier, and I think deserves a mention. So here it is!

45, rue de Babylone · Paris 7ᵉ
Tel. +33 (0)1 47 05 12 27
www.aupieddefouet.fr

L'Avenue
Café de l'Esplanade

It sometimes seems that all the beautiful Parisian avenues lead me to a Costes establishment. These are my two absolute favourite *terrasses* for breakfast meetings, late night after-dinners with unrepentant smokers, or simply soaking up the sun with a superb view.

L'Avenue · 41, avenue Montaigne · Paris 8ᵉ · Tel: +33 (0)1 40 70 14 91
www.avenue-restaurant.com
Café de l'Esplanade · 52, rue Fabert · Paris 7ᵉ · Tel: +33 (0)1 47 05 38 80

L'Astrance

L'Astrance was quite the Michelin trailblazer when it was awarded three stars in 2007, just seven years after opening – the first Parisian address to pick up the ultimate prize without the usual accompanying silverware and stuffiness. In their place – in a rather glacial part of the 16th – came a quiet, affable confidence from a young team, *en salle* Christophe Rohat and *en cuisine* brilliant chef Pascal Barbot, a former pupil of Alain Passard. In the first, crazy days of fusion spice overload, Barbot showed a true sensitivity towards Pacific Rim flavours when everyone else was piling them on. The original style remains, despite many imitators, though the cooking is now more floral and vegetal. The tall room and properly spaced tables make this a great place to come for an intimate dinner or peaceful lunch.

4, rue Beethoven · Paris 16ᵉ · Tel. +33 (0)1 40 50 84 40

The perfect little 'terrasse'... for eaves-dropping.

La Maison

Off one side of a cute little (round) square, La Maison's *terrasse* is where the *quartier* comes to catch up on the news, have a glass of wine and perhaps stick around for steak and chips. Very unpretentious, welcoming, with reasonably priced bistro food. Handy and off the beaten track, when all you want is a quiet, simple dinner, not to pretend you're a Michelin inspector.

28, place Saint-Ferdinand · Paris 17ᵉ · Tel. +33 (0)1 45 74 11 24
www.cafelamaison.com

Elegant
room,
impeccable
cooking.

Le Sergent Recruteur

As the control-freakish vogue for no-choice menus – with flimsy Japanese *omakase* justification – sweeps Paris, one needs to be pretty sure about leaving a large amount of cash and one's appetite in the hands of any chef. Antonin Bonnet wanted a restaurant, not a centre of gastronomical experimentation for chef or client, and he built it. The main room, with a few tables by the bar at the entrance for chic wine and tapas, is a delight, full of round corners, serene colours and gentle attentions. The feeling of being welcomed, settling in and being spoiled, so elusive to so many establishments, is perfectly mastered here. And the cooking of Antonin Bonnet, a former pupil of Michel Bras, makes sense of the tight, ever-changing, product-focused menu.

41, rue Saint-Louis en l'Île · Paris 4ᵉ · Tel. +33 (0)1 43 54 75 42
www.lesergentrecruteur.fr

From booking a table to ordering

The night is young – but it might not be long

Paris has adopted the rather annoying two-sittings system, either at 7:30 or much later at 9:30/10 pm, in many of its restaurants. The maîtres d's are a little less explicit in reminding you that you only have the table for two hours before the infinitely more important people dining after you arrive, than, say, in London, but be prepared nevertheless.

Always, *always* call if you cannot make it

There are no excuses. Unless they involve an ambulance or an undertaker.

Always check what sort of menu(s) the restaurant offers

As the vogue in Paris's hot restaurants is for the no-choice tasting menu – or often a *formule*, with simply a choice of fish or meat mains – make sure you know what you are getting yourself into. Especially if you have guests who may not be as adventurous as the chef would like.

Blackboard or iPad?

Ye olde auberge gimmick of a chalkboard with an ever-changing menu '*selon le marché du jour*' has been done and overdone. Still, it helps announce the style and feel of a place. Book-like velvet- or plastic-covered folders with four or more differently priced menus usually mean there are as many microwaves as commis in the kitchen. And call me old-fashioned, but I refuse, and shall always refuse, to order my tea on an iPad.

Menu du jour or *menu dégustation?*

The best-value *menus du jour* are often served at lunchtime. I tend to avoid the grand tasting menus – unless the chef is Japanese and integrates the idea of taking care of your stomach and digestion throughout the meal, not just filling you up and bombarding your palate.

Produits de saison or chef's speciality?

As a rule of thumb, if the chef's signature dish involves, say, Perigord truffles, it's best to avoid it in July. At the same time, the arrival of the first morilles, cèpes, lamb sweetbreads or the short season of mirabelle plums should not be missed. Very often, in the more traditional bistros, when the chef has scored some of these magical products, they are cooked very simply, and it would be a shame not to try them perfectly prepared and at their prime.

Please arrive hungry

It is the *moindre des politesses* towards a chef to arrive at a restaurant with a decent appetite. (The exception to this are Costes's restaurants, which is why the fashion and media industries adore them.) Portions in general are getting bigger and platoons of small 'tasting plate' menus are increasingly common, so much so that you'll be glad you skipped the macarons at 4 pm.

The world is not a soap opera

If your table is just for two, sometimes the noisier the room, the harder it is for neighbours to eavesdrop, while at other times there seems to be a sort of church-like alchemy happening between the flooring, the tables and the walls and you can hear every word. It's not always easy to choose the right place for every occasion. One word of advice, however – never end a relationship or propose marriage in a restaurant unless you are 100 per cent sure of the other person's reaction.

NO

Valet parking is not free

Even if no charge is stipulated, always make sure you have €10 (standard fee) in cash to tip the *voiturier*. (Paying a little extra means you don't even need to eat in 'his' restaurant if the one you have booked nearby has no such service. But keep that to yourself.)

Jacques Genin

Jacques Genin and Patrick Roger are perhaps the two most passionate-bordering-on-maniacal chocolate creators I have ever come across. Roald Dahl has a lot to answer for, but Genin is the closest I've ever seen to a French version of Willy Wonka. His huge, luxurious Marais boutique, with the workshop above (I've seen chocolate ganache made there and will *never* forget it), seemed a crazy folly when he first opened but the sheer brilliance and quality of his work has kept it standing – and shining. As well as his masterful chocolates, the millefeuille monté minute served in the salon de thé and his mango caramels have to be tasted to be believed. There are just not enough words to describe it. Go!

133, rue de Turenne · Paris 3ᵉ · Tel. +33 (0)1 45 77 29 01 · www.jacquesgenin.fr

Des Gâteaux et du Pain

One would think that choosing and buying cakes would be a joyous thing, but in this store, looking eerily like an undertaker's from the outside, you need to keep your voice down and watch your step. There's hardly a smile from the *vendeur*, but who cares when in front of you are the most exquisitely made bread, viennoiseries and, oddly, tucked away in the corner, an impressive choice of cakes and pastries? Everything is beautifully wrapped and comes with strict instructions about transport and storage. Make sure you use the right door to leave ... or else. And no photos.

63, boulevard Pasteur · Paris 15ᵉ · Tel. +33 (0)1 45 38 94 16
www.desgateauxetdupain.com

Chilly atmosphere; divine cakes.

THE store
Paris was
missing.
King Ducasse
has done
it again.

Le Chocolat
Alain Ducasse

On the very rowdy rue de la Roquette, off place de la Bastille, Alain Ducasse and master chocolatier Nicolas Berger have converted an old garage into an incredible chocolate factory. There are over forty varieties of chocolate, mixing filled bars with percentages and origins, almond pastes and pralines, and a gorgeous coconut and passion fruit-filled dark chocolate bar. At last we move away from a jewellery and cosmetics approach and back to origin, process and pure taste. It's a hugely exciting game-changer in a chocolate world over-contaminated by the image of luxury, even if Ducasse's prices are resolutely haute couture, not prêt à porter.

40, rue de la Roquette · Paris 11ᵉ · Tel. +33 (0)1 48 05 82 86
www.lechocolat-alainducasse.com

Le Chocolat Alain Ducasse ↑

Poilâne

Who has not heard of this legendary and revolutionary baker?
His Harvard-educated daughter Apollonia gamely took on the *maison* ten years ago after the tragic death of her father, when she was just eighteen, and continues to keep up the world-famous quality and tradition.
The punitions, their little shortcrust biscuits, are perfect for dunking.

8, rue du Cherche-midi · Paris 6ᵉ · Tel. +33 (0)1 45 48 42 59
49, boulevard de Grenelle · Paris 15ᵉ · Tel. +33 (0)1 45 79 11 49
38, rue Debelleyme · Paris 3ᵉ · Tel. +33 (0)1 44 61 83 39 · www.poilane.com

46 Elizabeth Street · London SW1W 9PA
Tel. +44 (0)207 808 4910
39 Cadogan Gardens · London SW3 2TB
Tel. +44 (0)203 263 6019

Boulangerie Secco

Perhaps not quite in the league of the others in this section but I give it a special mention for the tarte au citron that is *chablonnée* (lined) with white chocolate to keep the pastry crisp. Also very good are its wafer-thin tartes aux pommes. I'm very ready to make a detour when they pop into my mind unexpectedly. Ditto for the tarte aux pommes with the exceptionally fine crust.

75, boulevard de Grenelle · Paris 15ᵉ
101, rue de Rennes · Paris 6ᵉ · Tel. +33 (0)1 45 48 35 79

Blé Sucré

No concept store or designer décor here, just an honest to goodness *boulangerie–pâtisserie* with the most divine bread and cakes. The madeleines, lightly iced with a sugar coating, are perhaps the best in Paris. The three signature cakes of *la maison* are: tarte Tatin, melting caramelized apples on a sablé (sweetened shortcrust pastry) base rather than the usual unsweetened shortcrust or puff pastry; the Vollon, a mix of chocolate sabayon on almond dacquoise and praline; and the more exotic Aligre, with pineapple confit and a coconut base flavoured with ginger, vanilla and lemon. Heaven.

7, rue Antoine Vollon · Paris 12ᵉ
Tel. +33 (0)1 43 40 77 73 · www.blesucre.fr

Good and simple,
simple and good.
'Nuff said.

Du Pain et des Idées

Ooh, the sacristain with its feather-like pastry and silky crème patissière and the bottom caramelized bit that stuck a little to the baking tray. Ooh, the escargot chocolat pistache. Ooh, the majestic sourdough 'pain des amis'. Everything here is unbelievably good. The antique décor in the shop is gorgeous. One of my top five cake stops in Paris.

34, rue Yves Toudic · Paris 10ᵉ
Tel. +33 (0)1 42 40 44 52
www.dupainetdesidees.com

La Pâtisserie des Rêves

There's a complete change of atmosphere here in the sweet, happy, fantasy world of Philippe Conticini. His very pretty, cleverly designed concept stores set the scene perfectly for the way he plays around with the traditional structure of French classic pastries. He's a master of creaminess, texture and unctuous surprises, and while he might sometimes get a little sniped at by skinny Parisians for the richness of his creations, I love the way he tweaks them. Particularly the Paris-Brest, where the praline flows generously from the centre as you bite through the choux pastry.

93, rue du Bac · Paris 7ᵉ
Tel. +33 (0)1 42 84 00 82
19, rue Poncelet · Paris 17ᵉ
Tel. +33 (0)1 42 67 71 79
111, rue de Longchamps · Paris 16ᵉ · Tel. +33 (0)1 47 04 00 24
www.lapatisseriedesreves.com

Du Pain et des Idées ↑

Rose Bakery

Cake that does you good. Thanks both to the extreme pleasure of how it tastes, but also the absolute quality of everything it's made with. The ingredients are organic and sourced ethically, and everything is made freshly on the premises. When she opened the first *café–épicerie* in 2002, Rose Carrarini, originally from London, came with her own interpretations of favourite British and American recipes. An instant remedy for homesickness – when it hits I cross Paris for Rose's carrot cake with cream cheese frosting, an Eton mess or a scone. Eating in is a bit of a battle, however, as the room is cramped and the service sometimes a bit grumpy.

30, rue Debelleyme · Paris 3ᵉ · Tel. +33 (0)1 49 96 54 01 / 46, rue des Martyrs Paris 9ᵉ · Tel. +33 (0)1 42 82 12 80 / 10, boulevard de la Bastille · Paris 12ᵉ · Tel. +33 (0)1 46 28 21 14

Be

Alain Ducasse's bakery and lunchtime snack restaurant Be (Boulangépicier) has thrived amongst the residents and office workers in this plush part of town. The bread is excellent, as are the little carrot and tofu salads, the quirky sandwiches (when they're freshly made) and, especially, the creamy passion fruit tarte.

73, boulevard de Courcelles · Paris 8ᵉ · Tel. +33 (0)1 46 22 20 20
www.boulangepicier.com

Pierre Hermé

No other pâtissier appeals so directly to the indulgence and desire part of my brain. When I fancy a pastry, it's always a Hermé cake I think of first. At the moment I'm torn between the tarte vanille absolue and the plaisir sucré. All other macarons, apart from Ladurée's, which he created anyway, pale into oversweetened oblivion compared to his milk chocolate and passion fruit or salted caramel flavours. His chocolates are fabulous, too, and his little sablés and feuilletés. Latest creations include soft, sugar-filled vanilla waffles and an Ispahan granola.

**72, rue Bonaparte · Paris 6ᵉ ·
Tel. +33 (0)1 43 54 47 77 / 39, avenue de
l'Opéra · Paris 2ᵉ / 58, avenue Paul Doumer ·
Paris 16ᵉ / 4, rue Cambon · Paris 1ᵉʳ /
185, rue de Vaugirard · Paris 15ᵉ / Selfridges ·
400 Oxford Street · London W1A 1AB /
13 Lowndes Street · London SW1X 9EX
www.pierreherme.com**

The god of pâtisserie. That's all there is to say.

Patrick Roger

These days, the crazy genius Patrick Roger is more often to be seen sculpting all sorts of weird, gigantic forms out of chocolate than making the incredible little *bouchées* we're lucky enough to get to eat. Most recently, he made an entire tropical tree, complete with life-sized chocolate chimps, as the centrepiece for his new store on place de la Madeleine. I love what he does with citrus fruits – notably his confit oranges in chocolate and the famous lime ganache.

**3, place de la Madeleine · Paris 8ᵉ ·
Tel. +33 (0)1 42 65 24 47 /
108, boulevard Saint-Germain ·
Paris 6ᵉ · Tel. +33 (0)9 63 64 50 21 /
45, avenue Victor Hugo · Paris 16ᵉ ·
Tel. +33 (0)1 45 01 66 71 /
199, rue du Faubourg Saint-Honoré · Paris 8ᵉ ·
Tel. +33 (0)1 45 61 11 46 / 91, rue de Rennes ·
Paris 6ᵉ· Tel. +33 (0)1 45 44 66 13
www.patrickroger.com/en**

Chocolate is his passion, and his modelling clay.

Gontran Cherrier

With his film-star looks (*gueule d'amour*), famous TV chef Gontran Cherrier had all the running to make when he first opened his bakery on rue Caulaincourt. Particularly when it comes to bread, it's not enough to be all over the press to keep the clients returning. Chez Gontran – sigh of relief – it's hip, it's creative and it's good! Special mention for his black-as-night squid-ink baguette and the genius rye flour flaky pastry on his galette des rois.

22, rue Caulaincourt · Paris 18ᵉ
Tel. +33 (0)1 46 06 82 66
8, rue Juliette Lamber · Paris 17ᵉ
Tel. +33 (0)1 40 54 72 60
www.gontrancherrierboulanger.com

Pain de Sucre

An impressively sleek façade tempts you with futuristic-looking cakes and ice cream. The creations are daring, and not always a complete success – perhaps they try to do too much, perhaps it's a little too gimmicky? But there's real personality and innovation here, and everything, especially the strange-looking eclairs, is worth a try.

14, rue Rambuteau · Paris 3ᵉ
Tel. +33 (0)1 45 74 68 92
www.patisseriepaindesucre.com

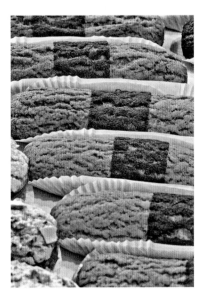

Carl Marletti

With his gorgeous boutique and brilliant cakes, Carl Marletti is a darling of the 5th arrondissement. Somehow he manages to keep his cakes feather light while intensifying their taste, particularly when it comes to the fruit in his orange and lemon tartes. The red fruit, rose and vanilla cream creation he dreamed up in honour of the nearby Cabaret Paradis Latin and his millefeuilles rank as his two most famous cakes.

51, rue Censier · Paris 5ᵉ
Tel. +33 (0)1 43 31 68 12
www.carlmarletti.com

Pâtisserie des Martyrs

Sébastien Gaudard has one of the most impressive pedigrees a pastry chef could ever dream of. Son of a famous Lorraine baker, Sébastien was Pierre Hermé's right-hand man, before taking over at Fauchon and then opening his own funky tea room at Le Bon Marché department store. Here, in his brand-new atelier and pretty, almost demure, shop, he's gone back to the pure classics, revisiting and 'de-sugaring' them as he goes. Baba, tarte au citron, eclairs and millefeuilles, Gaudard is inventing and setting a new standard all of his own.

22, rue des Martyrs · Paris 9ᵉ
Tel. +33 (0)1 71 18 24 70
www.sebastiengaudard.fr

Here's where you can reward yourself for scaling the heights of Montmartre.

The Parisian
sweet treatment
of exotic
flavours.

Sadaharu Aoki

A doll's house of a pastry shop, the décor is dainty, white and slick,
with a salon de thé leading from the shop for an instant fix. The usual
Japanese extreme courtesy and patience will be a godsend the first time
you come here as it is so difficult to take it all in and make a speedy
choice. I particularly love the one-bite-size slices of Aoki's fantastic cakes
and the green tea ice-cream wafers. His chocolates look more exquisite
than they taste and I usually stick to the eclairs, millefeuilles and
viennoiseries laced with green tea and sesame.

25, rue Pérignon · Paris 15ᵉ · Tel. +33 (0)1 43 06 02 71
35, rue de Vaugirard · Paris 6ᵉ · Tel. +33 (0)1 45 44 48 90
56, boulevard de Port Royal · Paris 5ᵉ · Tel. +33 (0)1 45 35 36 80
www.sadaharuaoki.fr

How to have your cake and eat it, too

Cake worship: a Parisian mania

Cake fancying has become an international sport, and guided cake and chocolate tours are very popular. You can spend a day being taken to the most famous pâtissiers' shops to taste and buy, and to photograph and even meet one of the growing list of stars. See pages 198–199.

Sweet neighbourhood pride – choosing your pâtissier

In Paris, as elsewhere in France, respect for the French artisan is at a high. Everyone knows the boundaries between the professional and the amateur are very clear when it comes to *la pâtisserie*. Every good *pâtisserie de quartier* will have its speciality – sometimes an old-fashioned 'cake de voyage', sometimes the pâtissier will be a wizard with meringue or have a secret when it comes to working his shortcrust pastry. Recipes and tricks of the trade are jealously guarded. Never mind the world-famous accolade Meilleur Ouvrier de France, even a mayor's prize for humble apple pie can make a man famous in his own arrondissement.

Some bread can pass for cake

Brioches and petits pains au lait are made with rich bread doughs containing butter and milk and can at times stave off the desire for something very sweet or buttery. The true killers, however, are les chouquettes, little bite-sized choux pastries studded with white sugar, crisp on the outside, wet and melting within. They often sit in innocent baskets beside the viennoiseries, and it is impossible to eat only one.

A Sweet Year

The fashionable bûche de Noël

Serving a designer 'bûche' at Christmas, something from Pierre Hermé's* new collection, or the signature cake from Paris's latest baking *chéri*, will bring you as much, if not more, admiration than slaving over homemade macarons. The Christmas bûche display starts around the end of October and the most sought after will sell out fast.

La galette des rois: the timing's off
Hot on the heels of la bûche de Noël comes la galette des rois at Epiphany. A flat puff pastry pie, it has a traditional frangipane filling (kirsch-flavoured, eggy, almond paste), apple (not bad) and chocolate (OK in a tiny sliver), or the hairshirt dry version, which is plain pastry, and (unless it is the superlative version from Poilâne) in my opinion should not be wished on your worst enemy.

Crêpes in February!
Twice! Once at the fête de la Chandeleur and again at Mardi Gras, where they are joined by seemingly hundreds of versions of fried dough deliciously dusted in sugar.

Le coup de grâce: chocolate bunnies and ... mussels?
Easter chocolates are terribly civilized in France, I find, compared to those of my Irish childhood. Eggs remain reasonably small, the hideous commercial chocolate eggs haven't quite taken over yet and real chocolatiers' art is proudly on show. The odd mixture in the line-up (all those chocolate lobsters and snails amongst the bunnies and eggs?) still makes me smile. After Easter, there is a distinct lull in the mighty sugary onslaught until the marrons glacés and bûche de Noël at the end of the year.

* See index page 203

NO

Having cheese *and* dessert is *so* yesterday
Only very rarely these days in Paris will you be served a full cheeseboard followed by a rich dessert. So if you are planning to produce a sweet masterpiece, simply serve a green salad after the main course, or nothing at all.

Other speciality shops

Maison Pou

One of those delightful retro shops where the queuing system can be baffling, so if you're British looking for some superlative pâté en croûte, be warned. This is where *le Tout-Paris* comes for the best choucroute in town. The foie gras and charcuterie are all excellent too. This store, nestled between big global high street fashion brands on avenue des Ternes, is a little time warp. A celebration of another era of French food (most of the clientele appear to be over fifty), an ode to aspic, a temple of prawn cocktail in grapefruit halves and suspiciously white sauce-clad chaud froid de poulet.

16, avenue des Ternes · Paris 17ᵉ · Tel. +33 (0)1 43 80 19 24 · www.maisonpou.com

Gilles Verot

Gilles and Catherine Verot have created a sort of fairy story from their *charcuterie*. For a start, they both look like film stars, and then their love for their produce and their business has brought them huge success in France and across the world, working with Daniel Boulud in New York and London. The best and most dedicated *charcutiers–traiteurs* in Paris.

7, rue Lecourbe · Paris 15ᵉ
Tel. +33 (0)1 47 34 01 03
www.verot-charcuterie.fr

The VIP room of saucisson.

Joël Thiébault

Joel's produce exploded into the limelight at the end of the 1990s, when chefs began to discover the incredible variety, taste and quality of the vegetables he was growing on his land in Carrières-sur-Seine, a few kilometres west of Paris. He has constantly experimented with vegetables from other countries, harvesting times and methods, and has developed unique relationships with chefs. Now he's a much sought-after adviser in a Paris where restaurants are working more and more with vegetables as the centre point of a dish rather than a mere afterthought.

Marchés Gros and Président Wilson · Paris 16ᵉ
www.joelthiebault.fr

Hugo Desnoyer

Another artisan with film-star looks and increasing fame.
The first butcher to make the French *Who's Who*, Hugo's shop
in the 14th soon became the supplier to the most prestigious
Parisian tables, including Pierre Gagnaire, l'Astrance and
L'Élysée. Special mention for his exquisite veal. And now he has
two cookbooks under his belt so everyone can learn how to best
handle his exceptional produce.

45, rue Boulard · Paris 14ᵉ · Tel. +33 (0)1 45 40 76 67
www.regalez-vous.com

Fromagerie Quatrehomme

My local cheese store for over a
year when living in the sedate 7th,
this, more than any pâtisserie, was
where my children liked to come for
a treat. So, often, we would forgo
dessert for a cheese *plateau* lovingly
made up (usually with an old comté
or two) with the help of one of the
sellers. In 2000, Marie Quatrehomme
was awarded the title of Meilleure
Ouvrière de France, the highest
distinction for any French artisan.

62, rue de Sèvres · Paris 7ᵉ
Tel. +33 (0)1 47 34 33 45
www.quatrehomme.fr

Fromagerie Quatrehomme ↑

The art of food shopping

Even a single slice of pâté en croute requires patience

The queuing system in Paris can be a true nightmare.
Traditionally those who serve you are not allowed to handle
money, so often you must take your receipt to a booth, where
you will find a crazy-eyed, fast-counting man or woman. Once
you've paid, you take it back to the person who served you,
by which time he or she will be busy with someone else and
you have to wait all over again. Remember, good things come
to those who wait.

Never miss a chance to taste before you buy at the *fromagerie*

Sometimes, in cheese shops, a taste of the cheese on display is
offered to you. Even if you are going straight from the shop
to a first kiss with the future mother/father of your children,
do not refuse, it is considered rude.

Sometimes a *boucherie* is also a *charcuterie*, and vice versa

There are strange demarcations between meat sellers. It's not an
exact science. A *charcuterie* might have some beef, a *boucherie*
will often have chicken breasts whereas a *volailler* usually sticks
to his birds. It seems, however, that le boudin noir transcends all
borders in some mysterious blood-loving consensus.

Flirt. It will get you everywhere.

Or, rather, do not be surprised when the sellers flirt with you.
It's all part of the show.

Cakes, never underwrapped

There is nothing more frustrating than a seller lovingly setting
your quiche Lorraine on a little square of cardboard, enveloping

it in a beautifully crafted pyramid of floral paper, tying it with
a plastic ribbon, making a perfectly balanced knot so that it doesn't
tilt when you carry it – only for you to tear it all apart just in front
of the shop because it's 1:30 and you skipped breakfast.

Every food seller in Paris has a cookbook in him

Unless you're very rushed, always ask how the seller would cook
whatever it is you're buying. They love to show off their knowledge,
and even if you've already decided what you are going to make,
you'll pick up ideas for next time. If you have half an hour, ask
the people in the queue too.

In Paris, politeness matters, even if you're only buying a cabbage

Always, always, say *bonjour* (preferably with a 'Madame' or
'Monsieur' tagged on) as you walk into a store. It might not change
anything when you do, but if you *don't*, you shouldn't be surprised
if your melon for Friday wasn't ripe after all.

Stick to what you know

A *boulanger–pâtissier* is almost always only good at one or the
other, not both. Either the bread is awesome and the cakes a little
coarse, or the cakes exquisite and the bread rather neglected. It is
very rare that both are excellent – unless there are two artisans
working together.

NO

Even if it is called street food, it's rude to walk with your mouth full

If you're over fifteen, it is still
considered rude to eat while walking
down the street, though, admittedly,
a chocolate eclair is a wonder of design
when it comes to easy scoffing.

↑ Chez Julien

2

Classic restaurants*

↑ La Fontaine de Mars

*
**Parisian
postcard cafés,
restaurants
and brasseries
with traditional
French dishes.**

Paris belongs to us all. The city's beauty
is so intense that it's impossible to resist.
As with New York and London, eternal
images of Paris are part of our collective
aesthetic consciousness. We all feel
we know it, even before we arrive.
The beautiful, iconically Parisian places in
this chapter are those that will bring your
imaginings to life then throw them back
at your senses a hundredfold. And even if
they don't quite match your original
mental picture, they will never disappoint
in their pure Parisian-ness.

Bring a book
and float back
in time.

Café de Flore

At the heart of French intellectual life since its beginnings in 1887,
the art deco walls of le Flore retain all their magic. 'Au Flore', the
unspoken codes of which tables and floors to choose, times to go,
what (and how) to order are instinctive to regulars, invisible to
outsiders. But unless you are dressed like a basketball player, the
hallowed red banquettes where Apollinaire, Breton, Camus, Picasso,
de Beauvoir and Sartre – to name but a very few – did their drinking,
thinking and writing are yours for the sitting. Entering this mythical
glittering world, I usually order a full-on tourist Welsh rarebit and
a glass of Ladoucette Pouilly Fumé – and will love forever the little
jugs and cups in which they serve the hot chocolate and coffee.

172, boulevard Saint-Germain · Paris 6ᵉ · Tel. +33 (0)1 45 48 55 26
www.cafedeflore.fr

Chez Georges

As you move back in time, down the bright, narrow room towards the clatter of the kitchen and into the bosom of French bourgeois cooking, make sure your appetite is in gear. The white-aproned waitresses will soon be clucking over you, wedged tightly on your banquette, sharing – like it or not – the conversation from the next table. Portions are, well, enormous. Communal pots of cornichons and crème fraîche zip from table to table accompanying herrings and rillettes as starters. Perhaps not the best place for romantic, lingering meals, but for a first night in Paris, and a reminder of how plain bistro food is done, it's unbeatable.

1, rue du Mail · Paris 2ᵉ · Tel. +33 (0)1 42 60 07 11

Chartier

Like eating lunch in a history book.

Opened in 1897 for Parisian workers, the egalitarian concept – a bowl of soup for €1 – remains unchanged, apart from a larger menu of simple French classics and a clientele more likely to consist of tourists and back-packers. But Chartier swallows them up and feeds them all under its stunning high ceilings. Before, you'll almost certainly have to queue. Afterwards, your bill will be scribbled on the paper tablecloth by your brisk and elegantly clad waiter. It's a good place for groups, especially with unruly children, as, in this noisy cathedral of French cuisine, no one will hear them scream.

7, rue du Faubourg Montmartre · Paris 9ᵉ
Tel. +33 (0)1 47 70 86 29
www.bouillon-chartier.com

Aux Lyonnais

Perhaps the best bistro in Paris, and certainly the best *bouchon lyonnais* (restaurant serving traditional Lyonnais dishes) outside Lyon. Alain Ducasse applied his expertise to this famous establishment in 2002. Already an emblem of Parisian gastronomic history, it would have been easy to rely on its reputation and the undying affection Parisians have for *la cuisine lyonnaise* to maintain a decent clientele. But although all the classics are right there on the menu (blanquette de veau, quenelles à la Lyonnaise, sauce Nantua), many have been subtly tweaked and lightened. When you go, make sure you're hungry enough to make it through to dessert. Then, give in to the double pleasure of the île flottante aux pralines rouges, served with a sliver of outrageously sweet, garishly red-pink tarte.

32, rue Saint-Marc · Paris 2ᵉ · Tel. +33 (0)1 42 96 65 04 · www.auxlyonnais.com/en

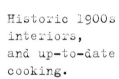

Historic 1900s interiors, and up-to-date cooking.

Café Jacquemart André

Of all Paris's museum cafés this is my favourite, happily, in one of my favourite buildings. There's something so soothing about the hushed atmosphere of the Musée Jacquemart André – such a contrast to the booming galleries of the hectic Louvre. The café, in one of the most sumptuous dining rooms in Paris, with a Tiepolo ceiling and Belgian tapestries, is equally genteel, although as they don't take reservations you might have to elbow your way through at lunchtime for their excellent salads. I prefer it, therefore, for the selection of tea and cake or their very good weekend brunch.

158, boulevard Haussmann · Paris 8ᵉ
Tel. +33 (0)1 45 62 11 59
musee-jacquemart-andre.com

Le Voltaire

Between the chic 6th and very chic 7th, close to Paris's most prestigious art and antique dealers, this place is always packed, and is a great favourite during Fashion Week. Voltaire did once live here, adding to one's sense of consuming a chunk of history with the famous 90-cent oeuf mayonnaise. This dish is really only a sort of in-joke, of course, and dinner for two is likely to hit the €200 mark if you are drinking wine (and you should). So brace yourselves, and who knows, as you devour your poached eggs with sorrel, beef fillet au poivre and tarte Tatin, you might be sitting elbow to elbow with Anna Wintour, as she picks at her perfectly steamed asparagus.

27, quai Voltaire · Paris 7ᵉ · Tel. +33 (0)1 42 61 17 49

↑ Café Marly

La Closerie des Lilas

Slightly off the tourist track, at the Port Royal end of the boulevard Montparnasse, this mythical literary haunt has remained a favourite place for writers and intellectuals to gather, and the *terrasse* is often dotted with big names and faded stars, for whom France always holds a table. There are two spaces, the brasserie and a quieter, more expensive gastronomic restaurant. I would always go for the simpler brasserie fare, especially as the service in both places can be erratic, to say the least. The tartare is the dish to choose, apparently, along with the very well-prepared seafood, but I love the flouncy desserts.

Flawed but still charming, like a favourite ex-boyfriend.

171, boulevard Montparnasse · Paris 6ᵉ
Tel. +33 (0)1 40 51 34 50
www.closeriedeslilas.fr

Café Marly

Designers Olivier Gagnère and Yves Taralon have transformed this former royal residence into one of the most spectacular places to people-watch in Paris. Inside, the restaurant is a succession of salons with plush décor and satisfyingly creaky floorboards and outside you sit comfortably under the arcades of the Louvre with a view over Pei's Pyramid, though chances are that the staff will destroy the comfort. Notoriously aloof, they know that all the effort has been made centuries ago and there is not much else they need do – even a menu and a *bonjour* are not always on their list. It doesn't matter. That is not why you are here. You know it, they know it, so relax, and even if your Shark (vodka, lemonade, grenadine) doesn't turn up for hours, you can quietly drink in the beauty. This is one of my favourite spots for a blissfully peaceful, 8 am breakfast outdoors after a (very) late night.

Palais du Louvre · 93, rue de Rivoli · Paris 1ᵉʳ · Tel. +33 (0)1 49 26 06 60
www.beaumarly.com/en/cafe-marly/home

Chez Julien

This is the 'other' Julien (less notorious than the splendid belle époque brasserie in the 10th), an ex-*boulangerie* whose 200-year-old décor was saved and made even more beautiful by Thierry Costes – *grand specialiste*, with the rest of his family, of the most stunning settings in Paris. And this one is no exception, with views over the Île Saint-Louis, a little paved *terrasse* hugging the pale blue façade on one side and wandering towards l'Église Saint-Gervais on the other. Inside it feels plush and glittery, and the food, while not threatening to take your attention away from your companion's conversation, is classic and impeccable.

1, rue du Pont Louis-Philippe · Paris 4ᵉ · Tel. +33 (0)1 42 78 31 64
www.beaumarly.com/en/chez-julien/home

Bright and
pretty by day,
so glam
at night.

For a taste
of the days
when travel
was an art.

Le Train Bleu

An improbable oasis, an exquisite *monument historique* just two flights
of stairs from the throng of the station below, Le Train Bleu is part of
a magnificent urban heritage from Paris's belle époque, now proudly
preserved. Eating in the restaurant – traditional French dishes,
naturally – is the best way of taking in the paintings and décor, although,
as with many entries in this section, the gastronomic experience may
not live up to the aesthetic one. That said, you can install yourself more
economically (with the dozy resident cats) in the leather armchairs of the
Big Ben Bar, off the main dining room. For a neurotic traveller like me,
the Big Ben and Le Train Bleu give the perfect excuse to turn up at least
an hour early for the train.

Gare de Lyon · Paris 12ᵉ · Tel. +33 (0)1 43 43 09 06 · www.le-train-bleu.com/uk/

Chez Jeannette

Unmissable. Perfect for aperitifs, a quick bite (cheese plate, pasta, baked eggs and foie gras or a simple steak), late nightcaps or for lazily spending an entire afternoon watching the film and media crowd from the *terrasse*, Chez Jeannette will restore your faith in Paris, despite the onslaught of a million Starbucks. The 1950s zinc bar and gorgeous ceilings are spectacularly *typique*, yet somehow you never feel as though you're in some kind of *Amélie* set. Laid back, friendly, always busy, it is the very essence of what makes Paris, well, Paris.

47, rue du Faubourg Saint-Denis · Paris 10ᵉ
Tel. +33 (0)1 47 70 30 89

Good plain
food and
cherished '50s
décor.

L'Ami Louis

When Louis received a bad review from *Le Figaro*, he stuck a copy in the window. Recently, the British critic A. A. Gill, writing in *Vanity Fair*, labelled L'Ami Louis squarely, 'the worst restaurant in the world'. So, be warned, expect anything. It could be wonderful, it could be awful. They might be charming, they might be odious, depending on their mood, the weather, etc. Don't ask, don't worry, it's not you, it's them. The only constant will be the deliciousness of the haystack of wispy chips you *must* order and which, tragically, always grow cold too quickly. Avoid the desserts, go for the roast chicken for two. Oh, and it is exorbitantly expensive, of course. Hurry up and go while Louis is still there.

32, rue du Vertbois · Paris 3ᵉ
Tel. +33 (0)1 48 87 77 48

Rosa Bonheur

Named after the famous feminist painter, Rosa Bonheur is a *guinguette* (open-air café) housed in a charming nineteenth-century pavilion, a place where people could come to eat, drink and dance. Tucked away in the Parc des Buttes-Chaumont – created by the architect Jean Charles Alphand for Napoleon III, and opened in 1867 for the Universal Exhibition – and accessible only on foot, it offers a canny way of making the most of this lovely park by night. You won't come for the food (tapas, snacks) or the wine, and certainly not to observe a chic clientele, but it's a gentle place to stop for tea or an ice cream after a picnic, and at night the sparkling lights and distant music will guide you to this unique, magical place where a more marginal Paris lets its hair down.

Parc des Buttes-Chaumont · 2, allée de la Cascade · Paris 19ᵉ
Tel. +33 (0)1 42 00 00 45 · www.rosabonheur.fr

La Fidélité

Easy, noisy, hip and decadent, this beautiful old brasserie, in a most unwelcoming street in a pretty unlikely part of town, is a wonderful place for late night (romantic) dining. Don't expect a gastronomic experience, it's more like something you'd cook yourself from Jamie Oliver for friends. But that's OK. I love the high, creamy walls, deep banquettes and low lighting. Afterwards you can dance, drink – and *smoke*, in La Cave below – or go upstairs to L'Appartement if you've been invited to a private dinner. Decorated in 1950s and '60s style, André Saravia and Lionel Bensemoun, kings of Parisian nights, created this private dining (and sleeping) space for those requiring maximum discretion.

12, rue de la Fidélité · Paris 10ᵉ · Tel. +33 (0)1 47 70 19 34 · www.lafidelite.com

La Fidélité ↑

'Le repas
gastronomique
français' is
alive and well.

L'Ambroisie

Another place where it is best to abandon any expectations of being
'pampered' by luxury service. At l'Ambroisie they will look you up and
down and dispatch you accordingly to the best or worst table. Then they will
wearily invite you to spend a small fortune on possibly the most exquisite
example of classical French cuisine in the world. In this hallowed corner of
place des Vosges the smiles and warmth are reserved for old money
regulars. But don't let that detract from your plate. Concentrate on the near
perfection of what you will taste (especially the snails, sweetbreads and
chocolate tart) and realize that this is the price to pay for the centuries of
superlative French cuisine that have passed within these tapestried walls.

9, place des Vosges · Paris 4ᵉ · Tel. +33 (0)1 42 78 51 45 · www.ambroisie-paris.com

La Fontaine de Mars

I've loved this place for many years. It was always a first pick when
we lived nearby and my family came to visit. It had great, hearty
south-western dishes for my rugby-playing brothers, lovely service
despite our hordes of children, and is so *typique.* Elevated (along with
the prices) after the Obamas' visit, the English menu gets handed
out as much as the original these days, but that's OK. The staff are
as charming as ever and careful and honest with their food. Try the
oeufs meurette and Christian Parra's excellent boudin noir with apples.
Or stick to the duck magret, confit and foie gras they cook so well.
It's particularly pleasant on a hot evening when the gentle sound of the
fountain seems to cool the *terrasse* a little.

129, rue Saint-Dominique · Paris 7ᵉ · Tel. +33 (0)1 47 05 46 44
www.fontainedemars.com/en/

Barack and
Michelle's
Parisian
pitstop.

Restaurant rules

There is no set dress code

Unless it's written down and posted outside the dining room.
Only a handful of haute-cuisine places, generally in the palace
hotels, require a jacket, a tie, no sport shoes, etc. But although
a confirmed reservation in any restaurant removes the need
to dress in any particular way, it is no guarantee that you won't
find yourself outcast if you don't look the part. This can happen
even more easily if you're overdressed rather than underdressed.
The answer? Have a style, any style. Then avoid eye contact and
wing it.

The *serveurs* are not your servants

They are doing their job, and making you happy is only a small
part of it, on a par with setting and clearing the table, keeping
the kitchen running smoothly, taking your money, etc.

Smoking is still OK (– ish)

Leaping up between courses to go outside for a cigarette as if
you haven't had one for a week, even during a €200 dinner,
is perfectly acceptable.

Six or more is a crowd

Tables of over six people are treated suspiciously by restaurant
staff and often end up in a separate room.

Clean your plate
This should be easy enough as portions, though getting bigger, are not usually supersized in Paris. Saying you don't 'like' it will not go down well. At best, the waiter or even the chef will be hurt, at worst, they may come over and argue with you and your pathetic, unworthy taste buds.

Doggy bags?
Nope, still not the way to go.

... But (some) doggies are fine
Small dogs, on the other hand, just like children, are fine as long as they behave themselves and are compact, clean, nicely turned out and emit minimal yapping.

High chairs are vile
Most Parisian restaurants consider high chairs ugly, antisocial, vulgar objects. If your child cannot sit still and eat like you do in a normal chair, leave him or her at home with a babysitter.

NO

No kissing, please, we're eating

It may be the world's most romantic city, but above-table PDAs (public displays of affection) in restaurants, involving lips, hair touching or incessant hand holding between courses/mouthfuls, are considered the height of bad taste.
Be discreet – or get a room.

↑ Coutume Café

3

The very best...*

↑ Legrand filles et fils

*
**A product,
a dish, an
atmosphere,
or something
that's different
and new …**

Now and then, a dish, a cake, or a fruit will leave an indelible impression on your palate and your mind, and from then on you will crave it. At times you just must have chocolate, at others comforting pasta or pizza, or sometimes only a steak, some sushi or roast chicken will do. Paris holds the answer to all your edible desires; here's a snapshot of mine right now.

Buying and sampling the best products

Anne-Marie Cantin

Invented in the French town for which it was named, this delight made of chilled cream and fromage frais is light as air and delicately wrapped in fine cheesecloth. You really need to be directly on your way home when you pick up one of these whipped marvels, to avoid spoiling.

12, rue du Champ de Mars · Paris 7ᵉ
Tel. +33 (0)1 45 50 43 94
www.cantin.fr

La Grande Épicerie de Paris

Speaking of cream, English clotted, double and single creams (along with decent bacon) are the products I most miss from 'home' and often the sole reason I will make the trip to La Grande Épicerie de Paris, which thoughtfully stocks at least two of the three, often in their buttery Jersey incarnations. Special mention also for the crème douce Sacré Willy they often have – a particularly thick, smooth cream that is unbelievably good with meringues.

38, rue de Sèvres · Paris 7ᵉ
Tel. +33 (0)1 44 39 81 00
www.lagrandeepicerie.com

Cooperativa Latte Cisternino

The foodie craze for burrata has swept through the mid-range bistro and brasserie menus leaving us all desperate to get some at home. As it's even creamier than its already creamy generator (mozzarella), cream-loving me naturally did not opt out of the rush. With four branches of La Cooperativa Latte Cisternino stocking excellent stuff, I'll never be bereft of burrata again.

46, rue du Faubourg Poissonnière · Paris 10ᵉ
Tel. +33 (0)1 47 70 30 36

Gustave

Chez Gustave, the salted butter comes from the island of Noirmoutier, the nougat from Saint-Tropez and the chocolate from Monsieur Henri Roux. Sitting on the border with the residential 17th, this handsome concept store caters mainly to the designer microwaves of the time-poor, euro-rich locals. It's all delicious, and definitely worth a visit. The staff are adorable and if your Rimowa is already full, you can scoff your purchases on the spot at the *terrasse* outside.

72, boulevard Malesherbes · Paris 8ᵉ
Tel. +33 (0)1 53 76 16 09
www.gustave-paris.com

Bellota-Bellota

A choice of at least three magnificent hams, at perfect tasting temperature, are hand-sliced to order in front of you in this little shrine to monomania. Great wines and Spanish groceries to try on the spot or take away.

18, rue Jean Nicot · Paris 7ᵉ
Tel. +33 (0)1 53 59 96 96
www.bellota-bellota.com

Épices Roellinger

It used to be a constant frustration dealing with the tasteless, spindly twigs that pass for pods on sale in *épiceries* and supermarkets, until starry chef and spice expert Olivier Roellinger opened a Paris branch of his Cancale and Saint-Malo spice stores, complete with a cellar full of over fifteen different 'crus' of vanilla. They're not cheap, of course, but what a difference this quality will make in your cooking! The staff will explain which type goes best with which dish (and when the store is quiet they'll give you a peek at the cellar too) – Ugandan with its leathery notes is best with fish, meat and red wine sauces, while the gourmet Madagascar 'grande vanille' has chocolate notes which come alive in a crème anglaise.

51 bis, rue Sainte-Anne · Paris 2ᵉ
Tel. +33 (0)1 42 60 46 88
www.epices-roellinger.com

Les Délices d'Orient

Perhaps not something for which you have frequent cravings, but still good to know where to go for anything (fresh or frozen, in fact) you may need if you're cooking Lebanese tonight. My children love their exotic fruit juices laced with jasmine, hibiscus and pomegranate.

53, avenue Émile Zola · Paris 15ᵉ
Tel. +33 (0)1 45 79 10 00
www.lesdelicesdorient.com

Workshop Issé

There's a rather daunting collection of Japanese products in this very prettily accessorized canteen, just screaming at me to take some Japanese cooking classes. They serve really good-value set lunches around two communal tables, and the selection of fresh miso, soy sauce, dried fish flakes and yuzu juice (the only products I know what to do with at the moment) is excellent.

11, rue Saint-Augustin · Paris 2ᵉ
Tel. +33 (0)1 42 96 26 74

G. Detou

As much an institution for ingredients amongst serious amateur and professional chefs as Dehillerin and Mora are for equipment, this store is crammed with an incredible range of produce and is refreshingly devoid of any lifestyle schtick or attempt at cool gourmet display.

58, rue Tiquetonne · Paris 2ᵉ
Tel. +33 (0)1 42 33 96 43
www.gdetou.com

Legrand filles et fils

At the broad, beautiful entrance of the sublime Galerie Vivienne, between the glass ceiling and the swirling blue tiles, sits Legrand, one of the oldest and most knowledgeable wine stores (and *épiceries*) in Paris. You can nibble at some charcuterie while tasting a glass or two at the high bar, surrounded by hundreds of bottles to arrange in your imaginary cellar.

1, rue de la Banque · Paris 2ᵉ
Tel. +33 (0)1 42 60 07 12
www.caves-legrand.com

Le Rubis

Rough and ready just doesn't cover it. Do not expect to be mollycoddled here as you sit your glass on the barrels outside. Full of suits at lunchtime. The food is extremely basic but perfectly functional. Good on a bad-hair day.

10, rue du Marché Saint-Honoré · Paris 1ᵉʳ
Tel. +33 (0)1 42 61 03 34

Legrand filles et fils ↑

↑ Vivant Table

Verjus

A New Yorker supper club duo snapped up two gorgeous spaces right opposite the Palais Royal theatre. One's a restaurant and the other a more informal wine bar, where young Euro food hipsters flock.

52, rue de Richelieu · Paris 1ᵉʳ
Tel. +33 (0)1 42 97 54 40
www.verjusparis.com

TABLE - CAVE

Roseval

One of the most hyped addresses of the past year, I was a little disappointed by the food but enchanted by the wines. Erika, the Colombian sommelière, will guide you through the evening from the bar to the last course of the tasting menu with confidence and passion. The wine list is impressive, with many small producers from Sardinia and Italy figuring prominently. A Chablis l'Humeur du Temps 2011 flowed along perfectly with our meal. Notable names to go back for, Champagne 'Fidele' from Vouette and Sorbée and a delectable choice of whiskies, including Japanese Nikkas. With a couple of tables and chairs outside, it's a good place to make a few discoveries without being lectured at.

1, rue d'Eupatoria · Paris 20ᵉ
Tel. +33 (0)9 53 56 24 14
www.roseval.fr

Vivant

A great name for a restaurant, don't you think? After La Crémerie and Racines, this is another of beautifully tattooed Pierre Jancou's temples of natural wine, just next to Vivant Table, which is a restaurant proper. Both are musts when in the 10th. Disciples only, please.

43, rue des Petites Écuries · Paris 10ᵉ
Tel. +33 (0)1 42 46 43 55
www.vivantparis.com

Willi's Wine Bar

The regulars say that the revamp and opening of a large room next to the famous bar have spoilt it forever. For me, its appeal lies in the little non-tapas (thank God!) snacks served at any time of day with a decent glass of wine.

13, rue des Petits Champs · Paris 1ᵉʳ
Tel. +33 (0)1 42 61 05 09
www.williswinebar.com/en/

The art of enjoying wine

Champagne is ideal as an aperitif

Serve it chilled in flutes or wine glasses, not those retro *coupes* which let the bubbles escape too quickly, and *never* with ice cubes, no matter how many piscine cocktails you have enjoyed in nightclubs. It can be served throughout a meal if it is an especially festive occasion, although it's best to try to choose dishes that go well with it. Light, creamy, herby chicken and fish, oysters, lobsters and langoustines, truffles and foie gras all like the company of champagne. Lièvre à la royale, less so. I would avoid it completely at dessert, however, when the palate is tired and already laden with sugar.

Cooking with wine

If you are cooking with wine, as a rule of thumb, choose one from the same region as the dish and serve a similar bottle with the meal. Don't get too worked up about what goes in a marinade or the splash of white for cooking mussels or deglazing shallots for a beurre blanc – just use something you would be happy drinking, as you will probably be finishing the bottle. No matter what, do not buy the cheapest you can find because it's 'just going in the sauce'.

How many wines?

In restaurants, even with the most elaborate tasting menu, I find it best to limit the wines to two, maximum three, during a meal. This is easy to manage at home, where a wine can be served as an aperitif and continued through the starter, and even right through the meal – although it can be nice to bring out something special to taste during the main course.

Red or white, and how much?

If possible, stick to either white or red throughout the meal – your guests will thank you. Though you can vary them a little, always start with the lightest wine and remember it's better to serve something excellent and enjoy it slowly with the food than to continually fill glasses from more mediocre bottles. As is so often the case, less is more.

Pairing wine with food

Matching wine and food is at once a science, an art, a joy and a nightmare. At home, *you* can decide, and I wish you friends who love you enough to follow when you want to experiment and to forgive if you get it wrong. My knowledge is 'working', to say the least, and, at the risk of showing myself up horribly, I play it terribly safe. I have my old faithfuls, which I know will go down well with the type of food I serve. I always like champagne as the aperitif, as practically everyone loves it and it instantly lifts the mood. These days, I'll usually serve a good chablis or a light red from the Loire if there's a starter and then something from the south, like a Pic-Saint-Loup or Faugères (there are more and more excellently produced and reasonably priced wines coming out of Languedoc these days) with a meatier main course.

Continued overleaf →

NO

Never drink wine to quench your thirst

That is what water is for. Have a glass of water before a tasting or a meal, and also between different wines to appreciate them better.

Sweet endings?

As we become more adventurous with food, dessert wines are becoming increasingly fashionable. But if they are too sweet and heavy they can often be the nail in the coffin of a good night's sleep. At a restaurant, make sure the sommelier knows what state your appetite is in as you finish the evening, before taking his or her advice. I usually keep a Coteaux de Layon to hand if my guests insist on something new for pudding at home, and always an old Mas Amiel Maury or a Nikka whisky from the barrel for the inevitable chocolate dessert.

Tasting and discovering

Nowadays in Paris you can find a wide selection of excellent wines sold by the glass, and many bistros now seem to care about how and what you are drinking as much as the food you're eating. Always check the prices and have the sommelier help narrow down the choice. Don't let him go off on long speeches about his winegrowing friends, their vines and *terroir*, save that for the classes you may like to take some day. What's important to you, as you order, is the taste, in your glass, with your food.

It's on the label

A good bottle must have the name of the wine, producer and the year of its production on the label. If you've tasted something new you've liked, make a note of it or have the sommelier do it for you.

How to taste

When you are tasting, no need for dramatics or speeches. Never cup the glass in your palm; holding it by the stem prevents you from heating the wine with your hands or leaving unsightly fingerprints. Swirl the glass (more usually for a red, which needs a little air) quickly, with its base on the table, smell with your nose quite deeply plunged into the glass to check the wine is not corked, taste quickly and if there is no problem with the temperature have the sommelier serve without further ado.

The natural wine revolution advances

More and more natural wine bars are popping up where you can taste a glass of untampered-with, unique wine, and bottles are slowly making their way onto restaurant wine lists. It's always a surprise – sometimes a more pleasant one than others – and it's best to keep an open mind and a curious ear when tasting. But each one tells a story and their poetic labels and idiosyncratic names, such as La Mémé ('granny') for a wine from vines hundreds of years old, are often the best introduction.

Watch out for hidden extras

At a restaurant, things are at once easier and more difficult.
Unless you know them very well, and your budget is limitless,
never leave the choice of wines entirely to the sommelier. Be wary
of the opening line 'would you like to taste ...' as what appears to
be an invitation to discover something new free of charge will end
up on the bill. '*Offrir*' is the verb used when it really is a gift, and
even then there is no harm in double-checking, especially if you
are hosting and there are six of you.

Droit de bouchon (corkage fee)

As more and more hybrid wine bars, *épiceries* and *caves à manger*
(wineshop/restaurants) open, these three little words are popping
up on blackboards and may cause confusion. They refer to the
surcharge for opening and serving a bottle on the premises on top
of the price for simply buying and taking it away. Bringing your
own bottle to restaurants is uncommon but if you do, you will
(understandably) be charged, to make up a little for not choosing
from the wine list.

NO

Don't be bullied

If the sommelier is filling
your glasses too slowly (annoying)
or too quickly (even worse), tell him (or her).
Don't suffer in silence.
And, no, you are not obliged to buy
bottled water in Parisian restaurants,
no matter how insistently
the waiter asks,
'still or sparkling?'

Onion tart

Itinéraires

At the restaurant Itinéraires, Sylvain Sendra's tarte à l'oignon with seared foie gras, button mushrooms and nutmeg, teamed with an Alsace wine from Domaine Agapé (selected by Sylvain's wife, Sarah, the sommelière), is a sheer delight. Great value lunch menus and flexible tasting options for dinner make this an easy, cosy address.

5, rue de Pontoise · Paris 5ᵉ
Tel. +33 (0)1 46 33 60 11
www.restaurantitineraires.com

Scrambled eggs

Carette

The rich and creamy scrambled eggs come with tomatoes, ham, fines herbes or cheese and, best of all, their cheese puff pastry straws. Super for brunch or a *petite dînette*.

25, place des Vosges · Paris 3ᵉ
Tel. +33 (0)1 48 87 94 07
www.carette-paris.com/uk/

Oysters

Huitrerie Régis

Along with steak and chocolate, the desire for oysters when it strikes is one of the most imperious I know. They're very good here – oysters from Marennes-Oléron are all they serve – with excellent bread and wine to eat in or, if you can't nab a table (there are no reservations), to take away or have delivered.

3, rue de Montfaucon · Paris 6ᵉ
Tel. +33 (0)1 44 41 10 07
www.huitrerieregis.com

Chicken

Le Coq Rico

A monument to chicken, set high on Montmartre, with an entire wall covered with an impressive rôtisserie, and a bar behind which you can watch your bird brown. There are more traditional tables a little further into the room. It's not cheap, but the intense chicken jus, plump, fresh flesh and French fries will satisfy my most

Pascade

Cross Paris for a pascade? If the chef weren't Alexandre Bourdas (two Michelin stars at his SaQuaNa in Honfleur) it's possible that no one would have paid attention to his brave almost-a-crêperie concept. A pascade is a type of souffléd crêpe from Averyron. Bourdas makes them sweet, savoury – and delicious. For a quick lunch filled with good things, it's perfect.

14, rue Daunou · Paris 2e
Tel. +33 (0)1 42 60 11 00
pascade-alexandre-bourdas.com

powerful craving. Excellent desserts, including an unforgettably monumental millefeuille au chocolat.

98, rue Lepic · Paris 18e
Tel. +33 (0)1 42 59 82 89
www.lecoqrico.com/en/

Steak

Le Severo

For many years this has been *the* place in Paris for superlative beef. Directly supplied by Hugo Desnoyer, whose butcher's shop is just round the corner, *le patron*, William Bernet, is chef and butcher, preparing and hanging his meat in the basement of the restaurant. He seems a tad weary these days – the beef all comes from Germany (albeit via Hugo) to ensure consistency – but you might still find yourself sitting next to Catherine Deneuve.

8, rue des Plantes · Paris 14e
Tel. +33 (0)1 45 40 40 91

Boco

Food journalist Vincent Ferniot and his brother have cooked up a natty food concept where starry chefs create gorgeous dishes in cute jars, to eat in or take away. Deliciously mushy. Especially the rice pudding with orange caramel.

3, rue Danielle Casanova · Paris 1er
Tel. +33 (0)1 42 61 17 67
www.boco.fr

Crêpes

Breizh Café

In 2007 Bertrand Larcher from Cancale brought the Breton air to Paris after opening a crêperie in… Tokyo. Since then, this has been the place to go when you want to be sure of the origin of everything in and on your crêpe, from the blé noir (buckwheat) flour to the last scrap of andouille to the gooey loveliness of his incomparable salted caramel.

109, rue Vieille du Temple · Paris 3ᵉ
Tel. +33 (0)1 42 72 13 77
www.breizhcafe.com

Sandwiches

Restaurant Michel Rostang

The little masterpiece of luxury that is the truffle sandwich, at once rustic and ultra-sophisticated, is now available on order from Rostang's restaurants or from La Grande Épicerie de Paris while the French season lasts and the superior melanosporum are available. The sandwich comes in a cloth pouch with strict instructions about how best to serve the 25g (just under 1 oz.) of precious truffle nestling gloriously between slices of toasted pain de campagne au levain and salted butter.

20, rue Rennequin · Paris 17ᵉ
Tel. +33 (0)1 47 63 40 77
www.michelrostang.com

Chez Aline

The wife of rockstar chef Inaki Aizpitarte did not design a range of kids' clothes or write a yummy-mummy cookbook. Instead she learnt to run a professional kitchen and then opened a *sandwicherie* in this tiny ex-horse butcher's shop. It's in the same spirit as L'Épicerie du Verre Volé (see below), only with a slightly more Italo-Basque leaning and sympathetic to the sweet-toothed.

85, rue de la Roquette · Paris 11ᵉ
Tel. +33 (0)1 43 71 90 75

L'Épicerie du Verre Volé

Take all the most hyped ham, saucisson, cheese and oil names of the moment (including our friend Casanova from La Tête dans les Olives), squeeze their wares between slices of Thierry Breton's bread and you get one of the best sandwiches of your life! This welcome new trend is a breath of fresh air in a Paris overrun with sweet, soft, industrial fast-food versions.

54, rue de la Folie-Méricourt · Paris 11ᵉ
Tel. +33 (0)1 48 05 36 55
www.leverrevole.fr

Chez Aline ↑

Gosselin

Much more traditional, this pristine shop can be a bit hit or miss, but the jambon beurre regularly makes it into the Paris best sandwich polls. There are three Gosselins in the city, so it's a handy name to know.

125, rue Saint-Honoré · Paris 1ᵉʳ
Tel. +33 (0)1 45 08 03 59
99, rue Cardinet · Paris 17ᵉ
Tel. +33 (0)1 55 65 11 55
28, rue de Caumartin · Paris 9ᵉ
Tel. +33 (0)1 47 42 08 03
www.boulangerie-patisserie-artisanale-paris1.com

Abri

Chef Katsuaki Okiyama joins the ranks of the new Parisian sandwich wizards with his awesome tonkatsu and cabbage creation, almost as tall as a Scooby snack, but which definitely merits taking more time to swallow. Look out, we're on the razor's edge of Parisian hype! But it tastes fantastic.

92, rue du Faubourg Poissonnière · Paris 10ᵉ
Tel. +33 (0)1 83 97 00 00

Coffee

Coutume Café

Part of a welcome new group of cafés for serious coffee drinkers, along with Télescope (see below),

Caféothèque and ex-Rose Bakery chefs' Le Bal Café. Here the beans have been lovingly selected and you'll definitely taste the difference in your gourmet espresso. The décor is industrial-minimal and the snacks have a distinctly Anglo-Saxon leaning.

47, rue de Babylone · Paris 7ᵉ
Tel. +33 (0)1 45 51 50 47
www.coutumecafe.com

Télescope Café

Another of the new crop of Paris's serious coffee roasters, grinders and brewers. There is a definite American twang about the tasteful décor and ambience in this place. They make the filter coffee with as much love and care as the espressos. And the cakes are good, too.

5, rue Villedo · Paris 1ᵉʳ
Tel. +33 (0)1 42 61 33 14
www.telescopecafe.com

Cafés Verlet

Breathing in the coffeeness as you open the door of this famous little wood-clad institution, you realise you have entered *the* anti-Starbucks. Take your time to really taste their lovingly chosen, roasted and ground beans (my favourite is Yemen Matari, whose 'buttery, honeyed, spicy aromas evoke Russian leather'), until the hum of the coffee grinder interrupts your thoughts or conversation.

256, rue Saint-Honoré · Paris 1ᵉʳ
Tel. +33 (0)1 42 60 67 39
www.cafesverlet.com

Tea

La Maison des Trois Thés

Perhaps the ultimate refinement as far as tea experiences go in Paris. Maître Tseung, the only woman tea master in the world, will guide you as you choose from her incredible selection of finest teas and discover the Chinese tea ritual.

33, rue Gracieuse · Paris 5ᵉ
Tel. +33 (0)1 43 36 93 84
www.maisondestroisthes.com

Pets de nonne

Be (Boulangépicier)

Never mind their excellent bread, brioche and pound-cake-type creations, Alain Ducasse's Boulangépicier knows how to deep fry. This is where I head when one of the children needs a mouthful of inexcusably sinful sweetness and a light dusting of fine sugar from head to foot. The doughnuts and, during Carnival season, the cute little pets de nonne (sort of doughnut drops) make us cross town again and again.

73, boulevard de Courcelles · Paris 8ᵉ
Tel. +33 (0)1 46 22 20 20
www.boulangepicier.com

Our daily bread

It's still *that* important
And I love this about Paris. '*Long comme un jour sans pain*' (as long as a day without bread) is the expression used to describe a sad, lacklustre day, and many Parisians will still buy their fresh baguette twice a day, as a meal without bread is unthinkable.

Rejoice in the taste – but hurry!
Government regulations forbid preservatives in bread. That is why it is still good and why bakers thrive, rather like bookstores, where similar measures have helped protect French culture. So, do not curse the fact that your baguette will go stale after a few hours – instead rejoice in this twice-daily miracle, and try to plan your eating around it like so many others do.

Your baker is happy to handpick *your* baguette
You can ask for a baguette according to how long it was baked (*très cuite* or *pas trop cuite*) and the sales person will rummage around helpfully as if you were choosing a diamond ring.

... or half baguette
It's perfectly OK to buy a demi-baguette. Paris, like any big city these days, is full of *célibataires* (single people).

You can order ahead
Once you're a regular, you can pre-order your demi-baguette *pas trop cuite*, have it put aside for you and jump the queue – just make sure you have correct change.

Prize winners like to show off
The annual competition 'la meilleure baguette de Paris' is taken extremely seriously and, once a baker has won, he will keep the distinction proudly on display in his shop window for years.

Pick your brand

The big flour millers have branded and franchised their flour and bread recipes. Some are better gauges of quality than others – La Flute Gana is delicious, rare, famous and expensive; La Banette, *bof*!

Spoiled for choice

Often you can choose between the whiter, fluffier baguette *ordinaire* or a superior-quality, more rustic-looking *tradition*. More and more, Parisians are opting for the latter as it will keep overnight if made late in the afternoon and strict rules govern its 100 per cent natural ingredients. Campagne is usually sold in round loaves, tastes slightly more acidic than a baguette and will keep for a couple of days. And many local bakers are producing incredibly innovative – and delicious – speciality breads, such as Gontran Chérrier's* squid-ink baguette or seaweed bread, the perfect accompaniment for oysters.

At the table

Surprisingly, bread plates are only provided at very formal meals. Don't cut your bread – pull off small pieces as you go along. Since Monsieur Bordier made butter so chic, it has become much more commonly served as a sort of mini *apéro* (to my delight). Likewise for fleur de sel and good olive oil.

* See index page 203

NO

Avoid the plastic-wrapped *'pains américains'* imposters

Bread has not escaped the Anglo-Saxon foodie onslaught, and the range of long-life industrial *pains de mie* (also sliced loaves, muffins, breads with special grains which are often full of sugar) has exploded in supermarkets.

Dessert

Hélène Darroze

Hélène Darroze's desserts, created in tandem with her brilliant Scottish pastry chef, Kirk Whittle, make me love dinners here right to the end. Special mention for his pairings of white truffle and mascarpone, pink grapefruit and tonka bean.

4, rue d'Assas · Paris 6ᵉ
Tel. +33 (0)1 42 22 00 11
www.helenedarroze.com

Wild strawberry sorbet

Berthillon

What is it they do to the fruit they use to make their ice creams? Chez Berthillon, you will often find the taste is purer and intensified where so many other ice-cream products are dulled by over-aeration and too much sugar. This couldn't be more true than for the legendary wild strawberry sorbet, even more expensive than the other varieties, and only available when the fruit is deemed of high enough quality. The pungent sweetness is marvellous, and the sorbet is studded throughout with tiny, whole frozen strawberries.

29–31, rue Saint-Louis en l'Île · Paris 4ᵉ
Tel. +33 (0)1 43 54 31 61
www.berthillon.fr

Pain perdu (French toast)

Le Chardenoux des Prés

Fluffy brioche baked in an impossibly creamy custard. A pillow of sweetness. 'Melts in your mouth' doesn't do it justice.

27, rue du Dragon · Paris 6ᵉ
Tel. +33 (0)1 45 48 29 68
www.restaurantlechardenouxdespres.com/en/

Sesame matcha macarons

Sadaharu Aoki

Matcha powder is an acquired taste and demands an understanding touch when used in cakes and chocolates. Sadaharu Aoki is Paris's undisputed champion when it comes to marrying French pastry traditions with Japanese ingredients. His 'Bamboo' is perhaps his most famous creation, a long cake slice, alternating nine layers of Joconde biscuit, chocolate ganache and matcha-infused cream and syrup underneath a stunning bamboo 'drawing'. Aoki experiments with matcha in many of his other confections. My favourite is the pain au raisins au thé vert, where the green tea notes are a little less present than in the macarons or eclairs.

56, boulevard de Port Royal · Paris 5ᵉ
Tel. +33 (0)1 45 35 36 80
www.sadaharuaoki.com

EY HÔJICHA MÂCHA PISTACHE SESAME CITR

Sadaharu Aoki ↑

International flavours

Steak and burger

H.A.N.D (Have A Nice Day)

Groovy décor, amazing fried chicken and burgers. All the good bits of US fast food, done well.

39, rue de Richelieu · Paris 1ᵉʳ
Tel. +33 (0)1 40 15 03 27

Beef Club

Much more grown-up, much more carnivorous and right on the global burger trend. The burgers will put (more) hair on your chest if the excellent cocktails haven't already.

58, rue Jean-Jacques Rousseau · Paris 1ᵉʳ
Tel. +33 (0)9 54 37 13 65
www.eccbeefclub.com

Asian

Miss Kô

It's a bit of a French national sport to knock Philippe Starck, but I love the man and the way he conceives his restaurants. Noisy, lively, easy crowd-pleasers. Miss Kô is no exception, with wild décor, even by Starck standards, perfectly located at the Champs-Élysées/Louis Vuitton end of avenue George V. Miss Kô serves a world food cacophany of sushi, gyozas, bubble tea, bobun and sake non-stop from midday to 2 am.

49, avenue George V · Paris 8ᵉ
Tel. +33 (0)1 53 67 84 60
www.miss-ko.com

Vietnamese

Pho Banh Cuon 14

There are plenty of other places to eat pho – places that are more central, with less of a queue – but when I want the real thing, this is where I head.

129, avenue de Choisy · Paris 13ᵉ
Tel. +33 (0)1 45 83 61 15

Miss Kô ↑

Kai

Very expensive but very well-executed sushi and Japanese basics. The seating is as uncomfortable as the clientele is glittery.

18, rue du Louvre · Paris 1ᵉʳ
Tel. +33 (0)1 40 15 01 99

Kunitoraya II

The improbable décor of dark wood and handsome ceilings, unchanged from its former classic French bistro days, seems an odd setting for such refined (yet unstuffy) superior Japanese cooking. Super udons and tempura. Good for a quick lunch or chatty dinner.

5, rue Villedo · Paris 1ᵉʳ
Tel. +33 (0)1 47 03 07 74
Kunitoraya.com/villedo

Guilo Guilo

A brilliant, theatrical Japanese chef and his team perform for you as you sit at a counter around their central kitchen. Glam and delish. And in Montmartre.

8, rue Garreau · Paris 18ᵉ
Tel. +33 (0)1 42 54 23 92
www.guiloguilo.com

Gyoza (Japanese ravioli)

Gyoza Bar

The gaudy, *franchouillard* passage des Panoramas seems an odd place for this rather stark, ultra-modern bar until you realize that the young chef is Shinichi Sato from the exquisite Passage 53 restaurant a few doors down. Outside, groups of tourists and visitors to the Musée Grévin across the boulevard file past you and your cute little gyozas (pork, ginger and leek ravioli, half-grilled, half-steamed) at the deep, comfy counter. That's all there is on the menu, served in eights or twelves with a cheeky beansprout salad and spicy sauce. Completely addictive and perfect as a speedy, late afternoon, pre-cinema or theatre plate of goodness.

56, passage des Panoramas · Paris 2ᵉ
Tel. +33 (0)1 44 82 00 62

Ramen

Naritake

Along with Kunitoraya's, Naritake's ramen are probably the best you'll find in Paris. The décor and menu are as minimalist as your bowls will be rich, warming and slurpy. It's tiny and crowded, only twenty-five or so seats, with a few along the bar looking onto the steaming cauldrons of bouillon. Best for lunch as evening queues can be insane.

31, rue des Petits Champs · Paris 1ᵉʳ
Tel. +33 (0)1 42 86 03 83

Kibbeh

Chez le Libanais

Another good Saint-Germain spot for late-night munchies. Open every day of the year until 2 am, there's always a crowd outside this little Lebanese takeaway. It's not quite 'gourmet' fast food in the style of some new places, but their sandwiches and mezze are top-notch and huge care is taken in the selection of their ingredients and the way they put them together. Special mention for the chicken charwarma.

35, rue Saint-André des Arts · Paris 6ᵉ
Tel. +33 (0)1 40 46 07 39
www.chezlelibanais.com

Italian

L'Altro

Decent, no-fuss Italian standards in the heart of Saint-Germain. Good for an early bite after an afternoon of shopping or when you have the kids in tow.

16, rue du Dragon · Paris 6ᵉ
Tel. +33 (0)1 45 48 49 49

Caffe Burlot

Moody and gourmand, with a club below the dining room, this place feels a little unlikely just off the Champs-Élysées, invaded by restaurant chains. Thierry Burlot's cooking is always smart and sensual.

9, rue du Colisée · Paris 8ᵉ
Tel. +33 (0)1 53 75 42 00
www.beaumarly.com/en/caffeburlot/home

Pizza

Al Taglio

Hand-made pizza dough freshly baked in massive squares to cut and take away or eat in, with excellent ingredients on top. It should be so simple and here, well, it is.

2 bis, rue Neuve Popincourt · Paris 11ᵉ
Tel. +33 (0)1 43 38 12 00
www.altaglio.fr/en/

Pizza Chic

Exactly what it advertises: chic pizza – with the prices you'd expect. But they are very good and, in Paris, when it tastes good, people keep coming back.

13, rue de Mézières · Paris 6ᵉ
Tel. +33 (0)1 45 48 30 38
www.pizzachic.fr

3

Gourmet breaks

Le Fumoir

An enormous loungy, New York SoHo type of place which probably should be out of fashion but manages to keep on buzzing. Nice bar/*terrasse* area in front of the cavernous restaurant. And it's great as a stopover on walks along the Seine.

6, rue de l'Amiral de Coligny · Paris 1er
Tel. +33 (0)1 42 92 00 24
www.lefumoir.com

Breakfast

Café Marly

The spot for an 8 am start. Snuggle up in the sofas outside and watch Paris get moving from one of the most beautiful viewpoints in the city.

93, rue de Rivoli · Paris 1er
Tel. +33 (0)1 49 26 06 60
www.beaumarly.com/en/cafe-marly/home

La Cantine du Troquet Dupleix

Much less romantic than Café Marly, but still open early. If you ask nicely they might even let you have a slice of excellent terrine from the lunch menu instead of (or even with) the bread and jam.

53, boulevard de Grenelle · Paris 15e
Tel. +33 (0)1 45 75 98 00

Hôtel Amour

Already a legend even before it opened. For brunch (eggs Benedict, etc.) slalom your way past the pushchairs and through the dining room doors onto a cosy and peaceful garden/*terrasse*.

8, rue de Navarin · Paris 9e
Tel. +33 (0)1 48 78 31 80
www.hotelamourparis.fr

Bob's Kitchen

An 'ethico-veggie' heaven, for when your conscience or your hipster mates say no to eggs and bacon. Super salads, smoothies, juices and tarts.

74, rue des Gravilliers · Paris 3e
Tel. +33 (0)9 52 55 11 66
www.bobsjuicebar.com

Le Fumoir ↑

Les Deux Abeilles

A favourite haunt of fashion editors having their yearly dose of carbs or those on their way to or from the Musée du Quai Branly. The welcome is as dry as the crumble is luscious. Décor a bit like my grandma's Irish drawing room.

189, rue de l'Université · Paris 7ᵉ
Tel. +33 (0)1 45 55 64 04

Atmosphere

For the setting

Restaurant du Palais Royal

Wonderfully comfy armchairs, pashminas and ozone-busting heaters will keep you cosy, even in autumn, as the sun goes down. The food is, predictably, forgettable and pricey, but reasonably fresh and simple. Mostly, it's a great spot to let the soothing magic of the Palais Royal's vaults and gardens take you back through time.

110, galerie de Valois · Paris 1ᵉʳ
Tel. +33 (0)1 40 20 00 27
www.restaurantdupalaisroyal.com

Georges

Make sure you do not need to discuss anything too important when booking a table here. It's impossible not to be distracted by the floor-to-ceiling glass panels and the 180° vista over Paris's rooftops. Particularly splendid is the *terrasse* on a summer night. *Attention*, the dress code is chic.

Centre Pompidou
19, rue Beaubourg · Paris 4ᵉ
Tel. +33 (0)1 44 78 47 99
www.beaumarly.com/en/georges/home

Aperitif

Au Vide Gousset

A typically cute Parisian café with an excellent bakery next door and a difference – everything tastes good. Lunchtime salads, evening Aubrac steaks, nicely selected wines, coffees and teas. A perfect stop for *l'apéro* after the office and before dinner Chez Georges across the street.

10, rue des Petits Pères · Paris 2ᵉ
Tel. +33 (0)1 42 60 02 78
www.auvidegousset.fr

Georges ↑

↑ Mini Palais

Tokyo Eat

Part of the modern art museum in the Palais de Tokyo, this is one of my favourite *terrasses* in Paris when it comes alive in late spring. Perfect for a break from the museums or lunch after the Alma market or the Eiffel Tower. Arty crowd you could spend hours watching, and trendy but forgettable food.

Palais de Tokyo
13, avenue du Président Wilson · Paris 16ᵉ
Tel. +33 (0)1 47 20 00 29
www.palaisdetokyo.com/en/lifestyle/
tokyo-eat

Saut du Loup

Sharing the entrance of the Musée des Arts Décoratifs, the cuisine here will not wow you, but on a warm evening it's a treat to sit outside with the Louvre on one side, the Tuileries gardens on the other, under the gaze of the Eiffel Tower.

107, rue de Rivoli · Paris 1ᵉʳ
Tel. +33 (0)1 42 25 49 55

For lovers

Le Restaurant de l'Hôtel

Probably the most discreet and romantic dining room in Paris.

13, rue des Beaux Arts · Paris 6ᵉ
Tel. +33 (0)1 44 41 99 00
www.l-hotel.com

Hôtel Particulier

I'm only giving you this address because the memories I have of it are so intense I can never go back.

23, avenue Junot · Paris 18ᵉ
Tel. +33 (0)1 53 41 81 40
hotel-particulier-montmartre.com

For the terrace

Café Étienne Marcel

Looking a little shabby these days perhaps, but still *fashion à mort* with its global menu and desserts from Thoumieux.

64, rue de Tiquetonne · Paris 2ᵉ
Tel. +33 (0)1 45 08 01 03
www.beaumarly.com/en/etienne-marcel/home

Mini Palais

Grandiose *terrasse*, almost rivalling Café Marly's, with the added bonus of a 2 am bedtime.

3, avenue Winston Churchill · Paris 8ᵉ
Tel. +33 (0)1 42 56 42 42
www.minipalais.com/en/

Flora Danica

My favourite spot for serious working lunches when it's hot in Paris. The green and white shaded garden and the Scandinavian food keep you cool, and you feel miles away from the hustle and bustle of the Champs.

142, avenue des Champs-Élysées · Paris 8ᵉ
Tel. +33 (0)1 44 13 86 26
www.restaurants-maisondudanemark.com/
flora-danica

For people-watching

Brasserie Thoumieux and Restaurant Jean-François Piège

Superstar, baby-faced chef Jean-François Piège rules over both the dark, noisy yet irresistible brasserie downstairs and the dazzling gastronomic restaurant upstairs, which was beautifully designed by India Mahdavi.

79, rue Saint-Dominique · Paris 7ᵉ
Tel. +33 (0)1 47 05 49 75
www.thoumieux.fr

La Société

Jean-Louis Costes transformed this already regal building into one of Paris's most elegant dining rooms. The food is pure pared-back Costes, the clientele smooth and sparkly. Dress up!

4, place Saint-Germain-des-Prés · Paris 6ᵉ
Tel. +33 (0)1 53 63 60 60
www.restaurantlasociete.com

Colette Water Bar

Still crazy after all these years. Thirty minutes in here with your eyes peeled (and iPhone camera on, if you dare) will tell you more about world 'trends' than a €2-million Ipsos Mori market research budget.

213, rue Saint-Honoré · Paris 1ᵉʳ
Tel. +33 (0)1 55 35 33 90
www.en.colette.fr/

Aux Deux Amis

Scarily hip, with fantastic wines and great tapas. There's a slight Berlinish feel about the left-it-as-they-found-it, formica-rich décor.

45, rue Oberkampf · Paris 11ᵉ
Tel. +33 (0)1 58 30 38 13

Anahi

A favourite with the Fashion Weekers, although not for the (mostly) Argentinian food (of course not!). The dim light from distressed walls and candles is kind to even the most worked-on faces.

49, rue Volta · Paris 3ᵉ
Tel. +33 (0)1 48 87 88 24

With children

Café Bonpoint

Chef Kaori Endo has brought the Japanese cool of Nanashi (rue de Paradis in the 10th and rue Charlot in the Marais) to this lovely space with its pretty garden. There are bentos for the kids, organic purées for baby and matcha cake for yummy mummy.

6, rue de Tournon · Paris 6ᵉ
Tel. +33 (0)1 40 51 98 20
www.nanashi.fr

Mama Shelter

Having had the experience of a family whose children spent most of dinner with their (bare) feet on the table (tut, tut, *tut*), I can tell you with confidence that this place is one of Paris's child-friendliest – Philippe Starck's playful mind has seen to that.

109, rue de Bagnolet · Paris 20ᵉ
Tel. +33 (0)1 43 48 48 48
www.mamashelter.com/en/

Les 400 Coups

A restaurant and mini-cultural centre specially thought out for children and their parents. The organic food is made freshly on the premises, there's lots of room for kids to play and run around, and there are often concerts and shows, too. 'Bobo' and cool, handy for the Buttes-Chaumont park and the Cité des Sciences de la Villette.

12 bis, rue de la Villette · Paris 19ᵉ
Tel. +33 (0)1 40 40 77 78
www.les400coups.eu

↑ Marché Raspail

4

Off
to market*

France   Joël Thiébault

Votre marchand vous invite à découvrir les légumes de

Betterave

"palette de racines!!!"

2,40 Euros la botte

↑ Marché Président Wilson

Even after twenty-five years in Paris, the
markets have lost none of their magic.
The choice, abundance and sheer quality
of the food remain supreme and although
it's an essential part of my basic everyday
shopping, each market trip is an outing,
an experience, and every time I learn
something new. I'm still somewhere
between observer and user, I guess,
but I love *all* Parisian markets, from
the scattered outside stalls that invade
Belleville streets a few times a week, to
the pomp of Saxe Breteuil, a sort of grand
and glossy food parade, which appears
to be held in honour of the Eiffel Tower
and gentle 7th-arrondissement living.

'Bon chic,
bon genre'.

Marché
Saxe Breteuil

When I lived in the sleepy 7th this was my local market, and every week
I would wind my way through the very chic ladies in mink, with their little
dogs and deadly shopping trolleys, spoilt for choice amongst such amazing
produce. This is a spectacular, elegant market, with the Eiffel Tower at one
end of the view, Les Invalides at the other, in the heart of old-money Paris,
and these people know how to eat – better, they know how to cook. As
usual, I learnt so much from simply eavesdropping on conversations while
waiting in line, even if a noisy debate did not strike up quite so easily as in
other, more animated *quartiers*. My favourite stall is the apple seller – from
Normandy, naturally – who will ask you what you are planning to cook
before selling you anything. Do not dare ignore her advice on the three
types of apple vital to the success of your humble compote.

Thursday and Saturday · Avenue de Saxe · Paris 7ᵉ

Marché d'Aligre

Perhaps the trendiest market in Paris, it is nonetheless one of the most thriving and authentic. Film and music industry people mix with locals and families, meaning the market escapes the rather rarefied feel you can get at, say, Raspail or Alma. Open every day except Mondays, the true gastro-chic products (especially charcuterie and oils) are to be found inside the pretty covered Marché Beauvau, while the usual fruit and veg sellers line the rue d'Aligre in front. After the market, the numerous cafés and bistros around (notably the famous wine bar Baron Rouge, with its barrels on the pavement) mean that you can easily spend most of your day here, buying, eating and talking about food.

From Tuesday to Sunday · Place d'Aligre · Paris 12ᵉ

↑ Marché Président Wilson

A market
between three
museums.

Marché
Président Wilson

Another extremely chic market, although you're more likely to bump
into chefs from the nearby luxury hotels than French pop stars. Make
sure you come early, as there may only be a handful or two of the rarer
produce, and chefs' eyes are sharp (if they haven't been tipped off
by the stallholders already). Here, I love buying fresh flowering herbs,
and it's my go-to spot for courgette flowers in season. La Boucherie
Olivier is renowned, and star fishmonger Jacky Lorenzo satisfies the
local luxurious taste for Breton lobster and Mediterranean spider crab.
The flowers are particularly sumptuous, and walls of roses, laid flat
in squashed bouquets, quickly diminish as the blooms are carried off
to the lavish apartments in the area.

Wednesday and Saturday
Avenue du Président Wilson, between rue Debrousse and Place d'Iéna · Paris 16ᵉ

Marché des Enfants Rouges

Definitely the cutest and most charming Parisian market, it's also the oldest covered market in the city, created from an ex-orphanage (the name comes from the red uniforms the children used to wear). You feel as though you're entering a little village as you wander past not only food stalls but also snack bars, cafés and bistros, slowing you down deliciously. L'Estaminet des Enfants Rouges is the best-known bistro, but you can also grab a crêpe or a good old jambon beurre at more humble establishments. And for when you want to take home but not necessarily cook at all, there's a great choice of *traiteurs*, including Lebanese, Italian, Japanese and Moroccan. Outside, the rue de Bretagne is also a foodie hotspot.

From Tuesday to Sunday · 39, rue de Bretagne · Paris 3ᵉ

Straight from
the producers.

Marché

Raspail

The most famous, most loved by celebrities, and most expensive
of Paris's organic markets. Compact, sitting between Sèvres Babylone
and rue de Rennes, Raspail has been serving organic and *bio-dynamique*
converts for over twenty years. Mostly made up of fresh fruit and
vegetable stalls, with plenty of dairy and a couple of organic wine sellers,
you can also find everything to keep your home healthily ethical and
GMO and pesticide free. Special mention for the delicious organic crêpes
from Michel Beucher to pick up and nibble while you browse, fondle
the pedigree fruit and spot the celebrities behind their shades.

Every Sunday
At the crossroads of rue du Cherche midi and rue de Rennes · Paris 6ᵉ

Shop at the market like a local

The early bird catches the fattest langoustines
Come early. Especially if it's Sunday. After 10:30 or 11 o'clock it is likely you will be seriously injured by an old lady's shopping trolley and endure heightened stress levels as everyone jumps the queue for the last marrow bones at the butcher's (see advice on trolleys below).

Perfecting eye-contact manoeuvres is essential
It's all about eye contact. At long stalls, there are often two queues, with half the sellers looking after each one. When you meet a seller's eye and he or she says *bonjour* (or not) and then looks away, follow his gaze to 'his' queue. That's where you stand in line. If he keeps looking at you expectantly, it's either your turn to buy or a chance to jump the queue.

Be prepared. Be strategic. Be efficient.
Try not to move up and down the stall choosing from here and there or you may start hearing your seller muttering under his breath, his complaining becoming increasingly expletive as he drags his feet along, following you and waiting for you to make up your mind. Make a first sweep and a mental note. Then get in line for your seller. If it's a combined fruit and veg stall, you're allowed one move as you start buying from the other section.

Parisian dogs can go to markets too
Dogs are fine, but remember the size limit is set at cocker spaniel or King Charles. Nothing bigger.

Steal me a grape – and no one will mind
It is acceptable to steal a grape or a mirabelle and try it without asking the seller. I have no idea why this should be. Do not, under any circumstances, try this with other fruit.

Market camouflage: dress the part
This is Paris, please dress respectably. Everybody does, as there's a very good chance they will bump into their bank manager or GP. Umbrellas are to be avoided unless you want dirty looks and to be sworn at every five metres. Get a coat with a hood or find an attractive rain hat, it will keep your hands free.

Shopping trolleys are lethal weapons.
Get yours, and get in training.
Trolleys must be pulled along behind you, not in front or alongside. No sudden swerving – and setting baguettes or bouquets on them horizontally is just asking for trouble. They are essential equipment when muscling into a queue at a busy stall.

It's a snap. In a snap.
If you are simply coming to the market to take photos, get there early and, even if you were born under the Eiffel Tower, pretend you are a tourist who doesn't speak French. Smile and point at whatever it is you'd like to snap and do not wait for permission to be given. You've got about ten seconds. Say thank you.

NO

Only touch
the produce if you're invited –
and be gentle
Sometimes you will be invited
to choose your own fruit and vegetables,
sometimes this will get you into big trouble.
Go with it. Poking, prodding
and squeezing is frowned upon –
unless you buy, of course.

↑ Louisélio

5

Entertaining:
Kitchen- and
tableware*

↑ Merci

*
**A beautifully
laid table,
a well-equipped
kitchen –
everything
you need to
host with ease.**

If you're going through an intensive foodie
equipment gathering phase, then Paris is
your paradise. Every little interiors shop
will have something to tempt you. After so
many years, my kitchen cupboards have
reached saturation point and I could almost
open a small shop myself. The places I go
these days tend to be, first and foremost,
affordable, and where I know I'll find styling
ideas for my books and see what the
designers are doing with the latest colours
and materials.

Le Bon Marché

Along with Barneys in New York, whose style and atmosphere it much resembles, this is my very favourite department store. It's rarely crowded to the point of becoming a stressful place to shop, especially in the houseware department. It's where I usually come when I have something modern and beautiful to buy or replace in my kitchen, especially cutlery, kitchen knives and cast iron or stainless steel casseroles. The selection is fantastic. Every year the always inventive, cleverly curated Christmas space yields more ephemeral creations for my table and my kitchen.

24, rue de Sèvres · Paris 7ᵉ · Tel. +33 (0)1 44 39 80 00
www.lebonmarche.com/en.html

Mora

Sometimes I'll need to replace something technical and specific, and the two legendary stores where you can be sure of finding anything – from snail tongs to 20-litre jelly moulds – are Dehillerin and Mora, in the heart of the historic market quarter, Les Halles. Dehillerin may be more picturesque but Mora does it for me thanks to its choice, efficiency and service. Here, the sales staff know every nook and cranny and, if you're lucky and they're not too rushed, will take time to explain how to use the equipment. I particularly like Mora for their amazing selection of professional chocolate-making equipment and moulds. They also have a decent choice of fancy cake-making glittery things for the cupcakers amongst you.

13, rue Montmartre · Paris 1ᵉʳ
Tel. +33 (0)1 45 08 19 24 · www.mora.fr

Love at first
sight for
a concept
store? Yup.

Merci

Warning: this store might severely damage your levels of
satisfaction with your current lifestyle. The enormous building,
sitting off the boulevard Beaumarchais and swirling around a
courtyard, is the fantasy loft we have all dreamt of since our first
trip to NY's SoHo. The space, light and materials used (or simply
exposed and preserved) in this extraordinary space will coax you
into a dreamy limbo between aesthetic delight and frustration
at wanting to change everything in your home, right now.
The tableware department is a good place to start, and there are
so many must-have, bang up-to-date items at perfectly accessible
prices that you'd be mad not to go for.

111, boulevard Beaumarchais · Paris 3ᵉ
Tel. +33 (0)1 42 77 00 33 · www.merci-merci.com/en/

If you love cooking, you come here. No discussion!

Dehillerin

La Bovida

A monument, *Ratatouille*-land par excellence, at Dehillerin it feels as if nothing has changed, or even moved from under layers of dust, in this legendary store for centuries. As I have to clean my own, I'm not a great fan of copper, but this is where serious copper lovers come for the ultimate French *batterie*. The quality is excellent and prices up to 50 per cent less than in the US. But I love the place mostly because it is still there. Reassuringly, it has managed to survive intact through the global onslaught of technology, molecular gastronomy, thermomix and silicone. Now it would seem, thanks to the global foodie revolution, it is firmly here to stay. The narrow aisles, towering wooden shelving and dustcoated sales staff make this an obligatory stop on any foodlover's tour of Paris. And even if it's irksome to jostle with mere tourists, it's worth treating yourself to, say, a new balloon whisk, just for the charm of having something wrapped up for you in brown paper. Further down the rue Montmartre is La Bovida, also excellent, and all around this area you'll find tableware suppliers, once exclusively professional, now serving the growing masses of domestic wannabe chefs.

Dehillerin · 18, rue Coquillière · Paris 1ᵉʳ · Tel. +33 (0)1 42 36 53 13
www.e-dehillerin.fr/en/
La Bovida · 36, rue Montmartre · Paris 1ᵉʳ · Tel. +33 (0)1 42 36 09 99
www.labovida.com

La Bovida ↑

↑ Sentou

Sentou

Fresh ideas and smart materials.

Opened in Paris in 1977, the first Sentou Gallery soon became a leading distributor of exciting designers including Yanagi and Nogushi. For me, Sentou is synonymous with Tsé Tsé, the pair of prolific and fiercely independent French women designers whose first exhibitions were held there. Their slightly askew bowls with gold- and silver-plated interiors made my chocolate and caramel recipes look utterly gorgeous in the photos in my first books and their wonky-sided gratin dishes still add a touch of prettiness to my kitchen every day. Now when I shop there, I crave the vibrant colours and fine lines of Brigitte de Bazelaire's plates to mix and match according to the food and flowers on my table, and Sentou's own serving cutlery.

26, boulevard Raspail · Paris 7ᵉ
Tel. +33 (0)1 45 49 00 05
29, rue François Miron · Paris 4ᵉ
Tel. +33 (0)1 42 78 50 60 · www.sentou.fr

La Cornue Galerie

A beautiful new space showcasing the magnificent La Cornue kitchen ranges. Architect–designer Jean-Michel Wilmotte has exclusively designed their elegant line of induction hobs.
The gorgeous and original selection of knives, butchers' blocks and leather accessories, designed for La Cornue, will stave off your longing until the day you possess your very own La Cornue range cooker. Here you can also enjoy demonstrations of classic French cooking organized by a *chef cuisinier.*

54, rue de Bourgogne · Paris 1ᵉʳ · Tel: +33 (0)1 46 33 84 74
www.lacornue.com · www.lacornueusa.com

Home

Autour du Monde

It's so difficult now to find an interiors store that is beautifully curated, reasonably priced and where the collections change frequently. I love Home for this – I know there will always be something affordable for my kitchen or table here. Very often pieces are full of humour without stooping to gimmickry. As the stock turns around so fast, the sales here are giddily excellent and that's when my purchases reach beyond the kitchen, as there are often one-off pieces of furniture and lovely fabrics and rugs. But mostly I'll buy serving dishes and cutlery, and utensils I may not need to use that often but which make me happy simply by contemplating their brilliant design.

**8, rue des Francs Bourgeois · Paris 3ᵉ · Tel. +33 (0)1 42 77 06 08
www.bensimon.com/en**

Au Bain Marie

Designer and stylist Aude Clément is a vital guardian of French *arts de la table*. Everyone involved in food, restaurants, culinary art and interior design, from Paris and well beyond, remembers her insanely beautiful, enormous store next to L'Hôtel de Crillon, full of sumptuous treasures from France's culinary past and the latest creations of the day. Now these are to be found in smaller, yet still fascinating surroundings in her shop in the 7th. From antique books, knife rests, solid silver duck presses to hand-painted earthenware and tin plates in new designs, this is the place to come and find out about French history and extreme refinement *à table* through the centuries.

**56, rue de l'Université · Paris 7ᵉ
Tel. +33 (0)1 42 71 08 69
www.aubainmarie.fr**

Caravane

Another discovery I made through the stylists and photographers who worked on my books – Caravane's tableware and fabrics. Often made from the most simple of materials – tin, clay, leather – and rough, natural weaves, they mix and blend beautifully with the more contemporary pieces I like to use. You'll find them dotted about the beautiful store in the Marais – whose main showroom is housed dramatically under a high skylight – and set higgledy-piggledy around the tiny Caravane Emporium on rue Saint-Nicolas along with tablecloths, napkins and other tempting objects which will undoubtedly make your life complete.

6, rue Pavée · Paris 4ᵉ
Tel. +33 (0)1 44 61 04 20
4, rue Saint-Nicolas · Paris 12ᵉ
Tel. +33 (0)1 53 17 18 55
www.caravane.fr

Louisélio

Just off the peaceful, leafy Square Louvois, with its rather impressive fountain, is Louisélio's atelier. Here, she creates her delicate ceramics to order for Parisians in the know. If she's in, knock sharply and she'll be happy to explain how she works and help you decide what you'd like her to make for you.

14, rue Chabanais · Paris 2ᵉ
Tel. +33 (0)1 42 97 54 65

The new home
of Asian
design
in Paris.

CFOC

For over forty years this was the temple of Asian *arts de la table*, and it was one of my favourite places to come for fabrics, objects and simple (mostly Chinese) tableware. But with the death of its founder, François Dautresme, in 2002, CFOC was becoming a little sad, dusty and deserted, sitting in the lofty Haussmanian avenues of one of Paris's most affluent districts. Now it has been completely transformed by architects Sarah Lavoine and François Schmidt into a sort of luxury Asian concept store, showcasing famous and upcoming designers, complete with a *très chic* Japanese restaurant, Yoko. Even if the atmosphere is now more Faubourg Saint-Honoré than markets of Saigon, it is stunning. No photos. Do not touch, *s'il vous plaît. Merci.*

170, boulevard Haussmann · Paris 7ᵉ · Tel. +33 (0)1 53 53 40 80 · www.cfoc.fr

How to stock a Parisian pantry

Preserved and dried goods
Mainly pulses (beans and lentils), sardines and mackerel in olive oil or with lemon. Then there's fish soup, smoked cod's liver, confit de canard. We love our tins, and Mason and Kilner jars.

Garlic!
And onions, shallots, bouquet garni (or at least bay leaves). The starting point of so many French dishes.

Crème fraîche and real butter
For just a spoonful here and there. Nothing beats the taste of the real thing.

Olive oil, vinegar and mustard
For decent vinaigrettes and mayonnaise.

Staple vegetables
Carrots, onions, leeks and celery at the very least, for the mirepoix at the base of many soups and stews.

Mild spices
Preserved lemons, Moroccan spice mixes and cumin are the strict minimum.

Good quality vanilla
In pods, paste or extract as well as vanilla sugar.

Good salt
Either fleur de sel or grey sel de guérande. The nasty whiter-than-white stuff is losing ground.

Tomato sauce
An Italian brand is good; homemade and then preserved is even better.

Ready-rolled pastry for quiches and tartes
What's more, it comes in circles and with baking parchment already attached. Indispensable for everyday cooking. In Paris they like to cook, but they're not slaves to the kitchen.

Kitchen essentials for cooking like a Parisian

Salade spinner

Cocotte en fonte casserole dish

3 good knives: paring, serrated,
chef's *couteau d'office*

Potato ricer
for old-fashioned purée

Food processor big enough
to handle crudités

Rubber gloves to protect hands
and nails

Crêpe pan

Moule à manqué mould
for the 4/4 (pound) cake

An ancient gnarled knife
for opening oysters

A deep china *plat à gratin*
baking dish

6

Into the kitchen:

Menus and recipes*

Menu

Homemade chocolate granola

*

Buttermilk pancakes (*not* crêpes)
with bacon and maple syrup

*

Homemade Nutella

*

Le 'Crumbeul'

*

Scrambled eggs with tomatoes
and piment d'Espelette

*

Quiche 'Lauren'

Parisian brunch

Brunch here is often a curious mélange of reinterpreted 'Anglo-Saxon-ness'. Like mayonnaise in sushi or cream in carbonara, it reflects a (slightly inaccurate) idea of how the French think the native US/UK version might be. And now that seed-eaters have emerged from the drearily packaged, organic health food ghettos to appear in the hundreds of increasingly sexy, healthy cafés, brunch as an occasion suddenly has real culinary scope.

Homemade chocolate granola

This easy and delicious North American speciality
is a snap to prepare and a great gift.

PREPARATION: 5 MINUTES / COOKING: 20 MINUTES

MAKES 4 BREAKFAST BOWLS

- 4 oz. (125 g) chocolate, chopped
- ½ cup (40 g) rolled oat flakes
- 1 tablespoon (5 g) pistachios
- 1 tablespoon (5 g) flaked almonds
- 1 tablespoon (5 g) pecans (or hazel-nuts or macadamia nuts)
- 1 tablespoon (5 g) coconut flakes
- 1 tablespoon (5 g) pine nuts
- 1 tablespoon (20 g) runny honey

Preheat the oven to 350°F (180°C).
Mix all the ingredients together. Spread out over a baking sheet and bake
for 5–7 minutes until the mixture turns a beautiful golden colour.
Give the sheet a shake so it doesn't all stick together and bake for another
5 minutes or so. Leave to cool.
Serve with milk or yogurt and fresh fruit.

Buttermilk pancakes (*not* crêpes) with bacon and maple syrup

Fluffy 'American style' pancakes are preferred over the traditional flat crêpes
at brunch. The buttermilk makes them beautifully bouncy, but you can use fresh
whole milk instead.

PREPARATION: 5 MINUTES / COOKING: 20 MINUTES

MAKES 10–12 PANCAKES

- 2 cups (250 g) plain (all-purpose) flour
- ¾ cup (100 g) sugar
- 2 teaspoons (10 g) baking powder
- 3 eggs
- 1 generous cup (275 ml) buttermilk
- 1 teaspoon natural vanilla extract
- 5 tablespoons (75 g) melted butter + about ½ stick (50 g) for cooking
- maple syrup and crispy bacon to serve

Put the flour, sugar and baking powder in a mixing bowl and make a well in the
centre. Break the eggs in and add a little buttermilk. Gradually beat in the dry
ingredients from the sides of the bowl with a whisk, adding the vanilla extract
and more milk as you go.
Add the melted butter and beat well to smooth out any lumps.
Leave the batter to rest for 20 minutes or so if you have time.
Melt the butter in a crêpe pan or frying pan and pour in small ladlefuls of batter
to make pancakes of about 3 in. (8 cm) in diameter, turning each pancake when
little bubbles appear on the surface (about 30 seconds). Serve immediately
(while continuing to cook the rest of the batter) with bacon and maple syrup.

Homemade Nutella

This tastes infinitely better than the real stuff – which may be a dangerous thing. Have a pot of its industrial cousin on hand for those who must have their fix.

PREPARATION AND COOLING: 20 MINUTES

MAKES 2 MEDIUM JARS (OF AROUND 9 OZ. [250 G] EACH)
- ⅔ cup (100 g) whole blanched almonds
- ⅔ cup (100 g) whole blanched hazelnuts
- 1⅔ cups (400 ml) whole milk
- 3 tablespoons (50 g) powdered milk
- 2 tablespoons (65 g) runny, mild honey
- 6 oz. (175 g) dark chocolate, broken into squares
- 5½ oz. (150 g) milk chocolate, broken into squares

Preheat the oven to 350°F (180°C).
Line a baking sheet with baking parchment or foil and toast the nuts until they are golden brown, shaking them around a bit so they don't burn.
Pour the milk, powdered milk and honey into a pan and gently bring to the boil. Take the pan off the heat and add the chocolates, stirring gently until melted.
Grind the warm nuts in a blender as finely as possible. Add the milk mixture little by little and blast quickly until smooth.
Pour into a bowl or jars, cool and serve.

Le 'Crumbeul'

Something sweet and crunchy, slowly subsiding into something tart and smooth – a simple principle for this basic crumble that the French have eagerly adopted. This is a perfect health-boosting halfway house between breakfast and dessert. Substitute apples for the pears or mix them if you wish.

PREPARATION: 15 MINUTES / COOKING: 35 MINUTES

SERVES 6

- 1 lb. (450 g) ripe pears, peeled, cored and sliced
- 2 ripe mangoes, peeled and chopped
- 1 piece of stem ginger, or candied ginger, chopped finely

For the topping:
- 1½ cups (175 g) plain (all-purpose) flour
- 1 stick (100 g) salted butter, very cold
- ½ cup (100 g) brown sugar (demerara or muscovado)
- 1 cup (75 g) rolled oat flakes

Preheat the oven to 350°F (180°C).
Put the flour, butter and sugar into the bowl of the mixer and blend until the mixture resembles breadcrumbs. Stir through the oats.
Mix the fruit and the ginger and put into a baking dish.
Top with the crumble mixture and bake for about 35 minutes, until the fruit is bubbling a little around the sides of the dish and the crumble is golden.

Scrambled eggs with tomatoes and piment d'Espelette

Piment d'Espelette is a mild pepper from the Basque country – more like paprika than ultra-hot chilli powder – used in the Basque egg and pepper dish piperade. So quite naturally it finds its place in this creamy, eggy, hybrid dish.

PREPARATION: 10 MINUTES / COOKING: 10 MINUTES

SERVES 4

- 10 eggs
- ⅓ cup (75 ml) single (light) cream or whole milk
- ½ stick (50 g) butter (optional)

- 3 tomatoes, skinned and chopped roughly (or a small can, drained)
- a good pinch of piment d'Espelette
- salt

Whisk the eggs with the cream and season with salt. Cook over medium heat in a non-stick saucepan, scraping the eggs from the base of the pan as they start to thicken.

→

→ Make sure you stop cooking before they look completely done and that they are still a little gooey (usually after 5 minutes or so). Off the heat, add the butter if you're using it, and stir the tomatoes through, letting them heat and break up amongst the eggs.

Add the piment and mix well, sprinkling over a little more and some salt as you serve.

Good with big chunks of sourdough bread, toasted or not.

Quiche 'Lauren'

....

Lauren is a fashion editor at *Elle*. She is a perfect specimen of today's young Parisienne, crazy about fashion, *bien dans ses baskets*, curious about other cuisines yet confident of her French food classics. Here's her quiche Lorraine recipe, served with a green salad and … garlic.

....

PREPARATION: 10 MINUTES / COOKING: 40 MINUTES

SERVES 6

For the pastry dough:
- 1 egg
- 2 tablespoons water
- 1 stick (100 g) cold butter
- 2 ½ cups (300 g) all-purpose flour

For the filling:
- ½ oz. (100 g) lardons (bacon strips)
- ½ cup (125 ml) single (light) cream
- 4 eggs
- Handful of grated gruyère cheese

Ideally I would make my own pastry: whizz all of the ingredients for the dough together, then squash into a ball and roll out flat. However, as often as not I'll use ready-made rolled pastry. I like the La Marie brand.

Spread the pastry, with its oven-proof paper underneath, into an 11-in. (28-cm) quiche or pie dish, pushing it well into the corners. Prick it with a fork a few times and then put another layer of paper on top, together with baking beans (pie weights) or lentils and cook it for about 10 minutes at 350°F (180°C) – that's what my mum taught me: always bake the pastry blind.

Meanwhile, heat the lardons in a very hot frying pan, with no added fat. While they're browning, whisk the cream and eggs and then add the lardons.

Pour the mixture into the tart base, and sprinkle over a little grated gruyère cheese.

Cook the quiche in the oven for 30 minutes at 350°F (180°C) until it's lovely and golden and puffed up like a soufflé. It's best cold, with a green salad and fresh garlic vinaigrette.

How to host a dinner party

Serve an exotic main course inspired by your travels

It seems that at every Parisian dinner I go to, there is a touch of perceived exoticism. Many dishes from ex-French colonies, like Moroccan tagine or poulet Yassa from Senegal, are easy to make ahead and taste even better when reheated.

The label on the ingredients is as important as the one on your shoes/handbag/watch

Every Parisian host or hostess will have 'their' addresses. And sometimes they won't tell. Butchery, baking, chocolate-making and fishmongering, all have their own *maisons de haute couture* somewhere in Paris.

Puff pastry (still) rules for nibbles

Allumettes, little roulés, feuilletés of all types are still on the menu in Paris. They're comforting, easy to serve, and puff pastry is fun to get creative with if it's a totally homemade meal.

Keep aperitifs gentle. Save cocktails for their own occasion.

Parisians are not huge drinkers at dinner and a cocktail with strong alcohol will often be viewed as potentially spoiling the food to come. Offer chilled champagne or the wine that will be served with the meal.

Cheese: go for none, a mega labelled cheeseboard or a single statement cheese. Nothing in between.
When a Parisian hosts dinner, the cheese is freshly cut, in whole pieces. It is very bad form to pull out the half camembert you started the night before. Putting together a good cheeseboard is an art, and cheesemongers adore being asked to give a hand. But a perfectly ripe, beautifully matured cheese served alone is all the rage these days – usually served with a sweet chutney or fruit paste.

If you're making dessert, keep it very, very simple, or buy it. Like cheese – no in-betweens.
One cake, tarte, little *verrine* or exotic fruit salad. No one will be hungry and no one likes to appear greedy.

NO

Never make your own bread

Bread is essential to the meal, but this is not where a Parisian host likes to show off his or her skills. Bakers do it perfectly well and have the proper ovens. The real skill, and best way to spoil guests, is to choose the best baker in the *quartier* and walk a few extra blocks to buy his bread.

Menu

Pan-fried foie gras
with miso sweet potato mash

*

Roast capon with buttered sourdough,
hazelnut and truffled
white sausage stuffing

*

Chocolate, coffee
and sweet chestnut millefeuille

*

Two exotic fruit soups

Christmas in Paris is something special. Somehow the city manages to resist tacky over-commercialization and every *quartier*, street and shop window makes an effort to be particularly glittering. Tiny morsels of luxury are on offer all around; truffles, foie gras, lobster, champagne and chocolates can be found not only at the best markets, but also in *épicieries fines* and '*chez Monop*' (the fantastic supermarket chain), making *le réveillon* a very easy occasion to pull off – when it comes to cooking – because there is every excuse not to do any at all. Often the skill lies in choosing, preparing and ordering the best products well in advance for your guests' delight. It's also perfectly acceptable to serve a feast of foie gras, oysters, cheese and bûche de Noël (from a renowned pâtissier, please) without even having to turn on the oven. These dishes, then, are great for Christmas Day lunch, or for a chic pre-Christmas or New Year's Eve dinner.

Pan-fried foie gras
with miso sweet potato mash

Foie gras, when cooked from its raw state, is a very easy crowd-pleaser.
A little goes a long way and, somehow, the urgency involved in handling
such a delicacy gives any dish using it a glamorous boost. Timing is key,
as is an excellent extractor fan if you are dining anywhere near the stove.
Have everything else prepared, your guests safely seated at your table, and
bring a little spectacle to your festive dinner.

If you don't fancy the mash, you can serve the foie gras with roasted spiced
apples and pears or make a spicy chutney with dried and fresh mango.

PREPARATION: 10 MINUTES / COOKING: 50 MINUTES (MASH)
PLUS 5 MINUTES (FOIE GRAS)

SERVES 6

• 6 sweet potatoes
• a little olive oil
• 5 tablespoons (75 g) butter
• 3 tablespoons (40 g) white miso
• 6 'escalopes' (ready-prepared or cut from a lobe,
  removing any large veins) of raw foie gras
• fleur de sel and pepper

Preheat the oven to 350°F (180°).
Cut the sweet potatoes in half, place them on a baking sheet, drizzle
with a little olive oil and roast for about 50 minutes, until they are soft.
Scoop out the flesh, add the butter and mash or process until they are
smooth and silky. Stir through the miso, check seasoning and keep
the mash warm.
To cook the foie gras, have lots of kitchen paper on hand and make
sure your guests' plates are warmed. Heat a heavy frying pan until it is
smoking hot and drop in the foie gras. Let it sizzle (wear an apron!) for
about 30–60 seconds before flipping over. There should be a golden
crust on both sides.
Transfer the escalopes to kitchen paper to drain off any extra fat. Then
season well with the fleur de sel and serve with a spoonful of silky mash.

Roast capon with buttered sourdough, hazelnut and truffled white sausage stuffing

This may sound a little fancy, but the skills required are no more than for your usual Sunday bird. From the start of the game season right through the Christmas holidays, I still find the choice of edible birds available in Paris astounding. Every species has its haute couture level breed or appellation, from the Challans duck to the Bresse chicken. If you are not French, you may find it horrifying that I do not go through the complication of ordering turkey from my butcher or buying it at a market. Well, not any more. They are so eye-wateringly expensive. For the last few years I have picked up a very top-of-the-range capon at my supermarket and spent more on what goes inside it. This stuffing is moist, spicy and crunchy – you can always stoke up the truffle levels with a little more than those already in the boudin blanc (white pudding/sausage).

PREPARATION: 30 MINUTES / COOKING: 1½–2 HOURS

SERVES 6–8 (WITH LOTS OF LEFTOVERS)

- 1 capon, around 6½ lb. (3 kg)
- breadcrumbs made from about ½ loaf of stale sourdough bread
- ½ stick (50 g) salted butter + 1½ sticks (150 g) for the stuffing
- 1 large onion, chopped very finely
- ⅓ cup (50 g) shelled hazelnuts, crushed roughly
- 3 boudins blancs aux truffes, sliced and fried until golden
- salt, pepper and a little thyme

Rinse and dry the inside of the capon. Set it in an oven dish and let it come closer to room temperature before roasting.
Preheat the oven to 400°F (200°C).
Mix all the other ingredients together and stuff the capon. Any leftovers can be wrapped in foil and cooked beside the bird.
Rub the skin of the bird with the remaining quantity of butter and season with salt.
Place in the oven, immediately reduce the temperature to 350°F (180°C) and roast for about 1½ to 2 hours, basting regularly. If the breast is cooking too quickly, cover with foil.
Remove the capon from the oven, let it rest on a carving board and collect the cooking juices to make gravy. Serve with chestnuts, green beans or Brussels sprouts, and roasted carrots and parsnips.

Chocolate, coffee and sweet chestnut millefeuille

A little bit fiddly, and you'll need some space to construct the millefeuilles, but it makes for an impressive finale to a meal and can be prepared well in advance.

PREPARATION: 45 MINUTES

SERVES 6

- 8 oz. (250 g) very good dark chocolate
- ¾ cup (200 ml) whipping cream
- 1 tablespoon (15 g) mascarpone
- 3 tablespoons (20 g) sweet chestnut purée
- 1 teaspoon coffee essence or 1 teaspoon instant coffee dissolved in 1 tablespoon hot water
- cocoa powder and icing (confectioners') sugar or grated chocolate to serve

Melt the chocolate carefully and on a sheet of greaseproof (waxed) paper shape into 18 thin discs, about 3 in. (8 cm) diameter, either freestyle with the back of a spoon or using a round pastry cutter.
Put them on a tray or other flat surface and leave them in the fridge to cool and harden.
Whisk the cream and mascarpone together, then spoon in the chestnut purée and the coffee. Mix well.
Build each millefeuille by spooning some coffee chestnut cream on a chocolate disc and setting a second disc on top. Add another blob of chestnut cream and finally a third disc. Repeat with the remaining chocolate circles to make six millefeuilles.
Sprinkle with cocoa powder and icing (confectioners') sugar, or grated chocolate, and serve with crumbled candied chestnuts.

Two exotic fruit soups

White chocolate and passion fruit soup

COOKING: 10 MINUTES / COOLING: 5 MINUTES

SERVES 6

- 7 oz. (200 g) white chocolate
- ¾ cup (200 ml) passion fruit juice
- 1⅔ cups (400 ml) coconut milk
- 1 stalk lemongrass (optional)

Break the chocolate into ¾-in. (2-cm) pieces and place in a bowl large enough to contain the liquid.
Mix the passion fruit juice and coconut milk in a small saucepan and heat gently over a low heat. (If you are using lemongrass, let it steep in the hot coconut milk mixture.) Pour the hot liquid over the white chocolate pieces and allow to sit for 3–4 minutes before stirring.
Serve warm.

Strawberry and lemongrass soup with vanilla mascarpone cream

A little time and effort required here to sieve the puréed strawberries, but it must be done. Wonderfully aromatic.

PREPARATION: 40 MINUTES / CHILLING TIME: 30 MINUTES

SERVES 6

- 1¾–2¼ lb. (800 g–1 kg) fresh strawberries, hulled
- 3 stalks lemongrass, chopped
- icing (confectioners') sugar to taste
- 1 cup (250 ml) whipping cream
- ¾ cup (200 g) mascarpone
- 1 vanilla pod (or 1 teaspoon vanilla paste, or 2 to 3 drops vanilla extract)

Whizz the strawberries and lemongrass together in a blender then push them through a fine sieve to remove the little seeds and tiny remnants of lemongrass. Sweeten with icing (confectioners') sugar to taste, pour into individual serving glasses and chill thoroughly.
Whip the cream with the mascarpone until billowing and mix through the seeds from the vanilla pod (or the vanilla paste or extract). Set aside, then use to top the glasses of strawberry soup just before serving.

How to be the perfect guest

Sending flowers before or after the dinner is a lovely gesture
But unless you have staff who look after that sort of thing for you, it's OK turn up on the night with a bouquet. Don't do the single rose with a long stem thing we all learnt about in our French school books with Monsieur Berthillon and Marie-Claude. (Good) chocolates are always welcome.

A carefully chosen personal gift is always very sweet
Currently the fashion is to bring something you made yourself. Just make sure it looks like it's from Fortnum and Mason. Tupperware you ask to take back at the end of the evening will not do.

Don't bring wine unless you've been asked to
Unless it's a very special bottle that you are not expecting to see opened that evening. Wine to match the food will already have been chosen. Also, it might seem as if you've just grabbed a bottle from your own cellar. Chilled champagne, however, is always appropriate and most welcome.

In Paris, even though you're invited for 8:30, dinner is actually at 9 pm
But after 9:30, you are very, very late.

Smoking is absolutely fine
As long as you're on the balcony or hanging out of the window while you're doing it, and you will invariably find a partner in crime. Don't get drunk. Especially if you're a woman.

Wait for the OK from your hosts before handing back cutlery at the end of a course
Sometimes the same ones will be used throughout the meal, sometimes they'll be changed after every course.

No need to go off in raptures about the food
A discreet '*c'est délicieux*' aimed directly at the cook will do.

NO

Never serve yourself twice
from the cheeseboard
This is an ancient rule of etiquette –
having a second helping suggests
that the food that came
before was not sufficient.

Do not overstay your welcome
If you see orange juice being offered
after you've finished your third coffee,
it's known as a '*fout le camp*',
or 'get the hell out',
i.e., it's time to leave.

Menu

Puff pastry allumettes and 'snails'

*

Crudités and dips:
Artichoke, preserved lemon, parmesan and garlic (or not) dip
Shelley's mango chutney dip

*

Two-bite *bouchées*:
Salmon and sweet chilli
Avocado with lemon, poppy seeds and salted anchovy
Pea pesto with kimchi and sunflower seeds
Radishes and walnut cream cheese

*

Little *verrines* of tasty velouté:
Potato, honey and Speck
Parsnip, apple and ras el hanout

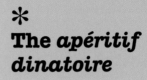

* The *apéritif dinatoire*

The much sniggered-at term '*apéritif dinatoire*' (basically pre-dinner drinks replacing dinner) has slowly crept into mainstream Parisian entertaining at home. The occasion has always existed, of course, just as '*l'apéritif*' *tout court*, as everyone knows that if you want to fill up at these things, you usually can; between the saucisson, olives, crudités and pretzels, you can make a meal of it. Now, the big difference is that guests, daringly, no longer make the move from sofa to around the table after drinks, and the coffee table (and also the carpet) has to take all the strain. Don't be fooled that this is a timesaver or less effort for whoever is doing the cooking, as individual portions, involving professional, caterer-level daintiness, seem to be more and more the norm. The following recipes are quite popular choices these days, reflecting the Parisian skill for satisfying not only appetites but tastes for tradition, flavour and design.

Puff pastry allumettes and 'snails'

The marvellous invention of ready-rolled puff pastry opens up many different possibilities to drop crumbs over yourself and your furniture whilst enthralled in your guests' conversation.

Allumettes

PREPARATION: 10 MINUTES / COOKING: 10 MINUTES

SERVES 6–8

- 1 roll of ready-prepared puff pastry (usually circular in form, though you can find packets of small rectangles)
- 1 egg, beaten.
- 2–3 tablespoons (20–30 g) small seeds: poppy, sesame, caraway, cumin …
- 2-3 tablespoons (15–20 g) grated gruyère, comté, beaufort or Swiss cheese
- salt and pepper

Preheat the oven to 350°F (180°C).
Cut the pastry into strips of about 4 in. (10 cm) long and ¾ in. (1.5 cm) wide.
Using a pastry brush, coat the surface of the strips with the beaten egg, then sprinkle with the seeds and/or the cheese. Add salt and pepper.
Put the allumettes onto a silicone sheet or baking parchment and bake for about 10 minutes, until they are golden. Remove and serve hot, warm or cold.

'Snails'

PREPARATION: 10 MINUTES / COOKING: 10 MINUTES

SERVES 6–8

- 1 roll of ready-prepared puff pastry
- 1 small jar of homemade or bought red or green pesto, or tapenade, or about 1 stick (100 g) garlic and parsley 'snail butter'

Preheat the oven to 350°F (180°C).
Cut the pastry into strips of about 4 in. (10 cm) long and ¾ in. (1.5 cm) wide.
Spread some of the pesto, tapenade or snail butter onto one side, then roll up like a snail's shell.
Put the 'snails' onto a silicone sheet or baking parchment and bake for about 10 minutes, until they are golden. Remove and serve hot, warm or cold.

Crudités and dips

They are still pretty much standard issue, as a nod to the figure-conscious – i.e. everyone, until the second drink kicks in. Carrot sticks and tiny tomatoes are now the cheesy Wotsits of the new century. No need to admit creative defeat, however, with these two dip recipes, which everyone loves. I have been serving them for years and they continue to prove wildly popular amongst my friends.

Artichoke, preserved lemon, parmesan and garlic (or not) dip

PREPARATION: 2 MINUTES

FOR A SMALL BOWL

- 1 small jar of preserved artichokes
- ½ a preserved lemon
- ½ cup (50 g) or so grated parmesan
- 1 garlic clove (if you so desire)
- pepper, to taste

Whizz all the ingredients with a little of the oil from the artichokes in a food processor. The dip won't need much, if any, salt but do add pepper. Good with flatbreads or pitta.

Shelley's mango chutney dip

From my friend, the astrologer and hostess extraordinaire,

Shelley Von Strunckel.

PREPARATION: 2 MINUTES

FOR A SMALL BOWL

- 2–3 tablespoons (40 g) good mango chutney
- ⅓ cup (75 g) fromage frais (or low-fat cream cheese)
- salt and pepper

Stir the chutney into the fromage frais and season with salt and pepper. Great with poppadoms, the thin and crispy Indian wafers.

Two-bite *bouchées*

Here are a few combinations for garnishing individual leaves of endive or baby gem lettuce. They are calorie-free and firm enough to keep their shape without disintegrating on the first bite.

For 10 *bouchées*, you'll need the leaves of a small lettuce or endive topped with any of the following garnishes.

Salmon and sweet chilli

PREPARATION: 10 MINUTES / COOKING: 10 MINUTES

- 2 salmon fillets, about 5 oz. (150 g) each
- 3 tablespoons (25 g) sweet chilli sauce

Heat the salmon fillets: either poach them lightly for 10 minutes in the microwave or bake them for a few minutes in the oven at 350°F (180°C). Break the salmon into pieces, spoon into the leaves and top with the sauce. Good warm or cold. (It is easier to prepare ahead and handle cold, however, so the leaves don't get soggy.)

Avocado with lemon, poppy seeds and salted anchovy

PREPARATION: 10 MINUTES

- 2 ripe avocados
- zest and juice of 1 lemon
- 2 tablespoons (20 g) poppy seeds
- 10 salted anchovies

Remove the avocado flesh and mash it roughly with the lemon juice and zest. Spoon into the leaves and garnish with a sprinkle of seeds and an anchovy.

Pea pesto with kimchi and sunflower seeds

PREPARATION: 10 MINUTES / COOKING: 5 MINUTES

- 1⅓ cups (200 g) cooked frozen peas
- juice of ½ lemon
- 2 to 3 tablespoons olive oil
- salt and pepper
- kimchi pickle (or any other pickle that takes your fancy)
- a small handful of sunflower seeds

Whizz the peas with the lemon juice and oil in a food processor. Spoon into the leaves. Season with salt and pepper and top with slivers of pickle and a few sunflower seeds.

Radishes and walnut cream cheese

PREPARATION: 10 MINUTES

- 3 tablespoons (45 g) cream cheese
- 4 or 5 walnuts (or pecans, hazelnuts or almonds, if you prefer)
- 5 or 6 radishes, washed, topped and tailed, and sliced very thinly
- marinated sardines or anchovies to garnish

Whizz the cream cheese with the walnuts in a food processor. Spoon into the leaves. Top with the sliced radishes and garnish with a little sliver of sardine or anchovy.

Little *verrines* of tasty velouté

Served hot or cold, soup is cool in Paris. It's also a good way of providing something easy to eat (drink) and reasonably substantial. These only take about 30 minutes to make – as long as you're not catering for hordes of people, in which case you'll want some help with the peeling.

Potato, honey and Speck

PREPARATION: 5 MINUTES / COOKING: 20 MINUTES

FOR 6–8 GLASSES FILLED WITH 3–4 SOUP SPOONFULS

- 14 oz. (400 g) floury potatoes, peeled and sliced
- 2 pt. (1 l) vegetable stock or water
- ⅔ cup (150 ml) single (light) cream
- 2 tablespoons (50 g) runny honey
- 3 or 4 slices Speck or other cured ham
- salt and pepper

Make cream of potato soup by boiling peeled potatoes in vegetable stock or water. Purée in a blender, then season with salt and pepper and stir in the cream. Garnish with a drizzle of runny honey and a couple of slivers of Speck ham just before serving.

Parsnip, apple and ras el hanout

PREPARATION: 10 MINUTES / COOKING: 20 MINUTES

FOR 6–8 GLASSES FILLED WITH 3–4 SOUP SPOONFULS

- 14 oz. (400 g) parsnips, peeled and sliced
- 2 pt. (1 l) vegetable stock or water
- ⅔ cup (150 ml) single (light) cream
- 2 teaspoons (5 g) ras el hanout spice mix
- salt and pepper
- 2 apples (or pears), grated

Boil the parsnips in vegetable stock or water. Purée in a blender, add the cream, flavour with ras el hanout spice mix and salt and pepper. Garnish with grated apple (or pear) as you serve.

↑ Le Royal Monceau

In the lap of luxury:
Palace hotels *

↑ Shangri-La

Step out of the real world for an hour or two and into a legendary Parisian palace.

So often featured on the pages of our favourite interiors, fashion and celebrity magazines, or in films and at festivals, images of Parisian palaces are easier to access than a seat at their exclusive bars. But they remain fascinatingly enticing, offering glimpses into lifestyles that intrigue and beckon. Paris's palaces are going through a mini revolution, as their clientele shifts and über luxury redefines itself. Here's a little guide to how to get the most out of the golden hues of palace life.

Raphael

Still classified as a luxury hotel, yet a far cry from the bright dazzle of the Mandarin Oriental or Shangri-La, there's a slightly faded charm to the Raphael that I love. Swathed in red velvet and dark wood, the lush yet cosy bar and salons are timeless and discreet and the rooftop terrace delivers gorgeous views over Paris. Used countless times as a film set, the Raphael has famously been home to Serge Gainsbourg and author-philosopher Bernard-Henri Lévy, and is John Malkovich's favourite spot for his frequent Parisian meetings and interviews. I wouldn't dine there, if I were you. Stick to breakfast, or cocktails, or secret nights in a lavish suite.

17, avenue Kléber · Paris 16ᵉ · Tel. +33 (0)1 53 64 32 00 · www.raphael-hotel.com

Four Seasons George V

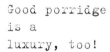

Good porridge
is a
luxury, too!

There's a two-Michelin-star restaurant here, under chef Éric Briffard, where gentlemen need to wear jacket and tie to enter the dining room. Such extreme decorum is not really my cup of tea. I much prefer dawdling over breakfast served in the long, sumptuous gallery – where you can choose to have your porridge made with milk or water, very rare in Paris – or a drink at the mahogany-lined bar, still one of the most loved and atmospheric in the City of Light.

31, avenue George V · Paris 8ᵉ
Tel. +33 (0)1 49 52 70 00
www.1.fourseasons.com/fr/paris

The most
dazzling
dining room
in Paris.

Le Meurice

Philippe Starck and his artist daughter
Ara completely transformed the
Meurice's rather sad interior in 2008,
and since then the Dalí 'brasserie'
has become one of my favourite places
for treats and celebrations at any time
of the day, as no one rocks a low sofa
quite like Starck. The main restaurant,
Le Meurice, steps up the sumptuous
décor another notch with Starck's
high silver consoles and ornate chairs
merging magnificently with the grey-gold
tones of marble and chandeliers.

228, rue de Rivoli · Paris 1ᵉʳ
Tel. +33 (0)1 44 58 10 10
www.lemeurice.com

La Cuisine and
Il Carpaccio:
the hotel
Le Royal
Monceau's
celebrated
restaurants.

← La Cuisine
Il Carpaccio ↓

Le Royal Monceau

Philippe Starck gets a lot of flak in France. Certainly his hotels can be a little design-heavy and the gimmicks can wear thin, but I think Le Royal Monceau, more understated, works beautifully. I'm a sucker for a comfy chair when dining, and Starck does a sofa-sided dining table *à merveille*. The dining room of La Cuisine is impressive, but the prices prevent it from becoming one of my regular haunts and I much prefer the clubby feel of the bar. You can slide into one of the camel leather sofas at any time and have an Hermé pastry to keep your exquisite china teacup company. There's an excellent design store with a great selection of books if you feel like staying all day.

37, avenue Hoche · Paris 8ᵉ · Tel. +33 (0)1 42 99 88 00 · www.leroyalmonceau.com

Le Royal Monceau ↑

Mandarin Oriental

Less grandiose than the Shangri-La, with an infinitely more modern take on its architecture and interior design, the Mandarin Oriental Paris was carved out of a protected 1930s building. Architect Jean-Michel Wilmotte, interior designer Sybille de Margerie and agency Jouin Manku have done a wonderful job transforming the eight storeys huddled around garden and balconies into perhaps Paris's most beautiful modern luxury hotel. Special mention for the sublime spa and pool, and Pierre Mathieu's delectable in-house pâtisserie, making this a real hotspot for cake and tea or coffee in the courtyard garden. The wonderful chef Thierry Marx reigns supreme over the rest of the food at the Mandarin in his avant-garde two-star Sur Mesure Par Thierry Marx and Asian-influenced Le Camélia restaurants.

251, rue Saint-Honoré · Paris 1er
Tel. +33 (0)1 70 98 78 88
www.mandarinoriental.com/paris/

Le Camélia, a modern masterpiece of cool and calm.

Parc Hyatt
Paris Vendôme

If you avoid Saturday nights, when the clientele is a little, erm, surreal, this is another great Parisian bar. Designed by Ed Tuttle, it's sexier, darker and altogether loungier than the George V, and a good place either to prolong an evening or to start it outside, with a cocktail on the *terrasse*.

5, rue de la Paix · Paris 2e · Tel. +33 (0)1 58 71 12 34 · paris.vendome.hyatt.com

Shangri-La

Set high up in Embassy-land, a stone's throw from the couture houses on avenues Montaigne and George V, with sumptuous views over the Eiffel Tower from a number of its suites, the Shangri-La was originally the residence of Napoléon Bonaparte's great-nephew, Prince Roland. First of the new crop of super-duper five-star palaces, catering to the world's mega rich, the Shangri-La drips luxury. I love the series of salons with podgy sofas and bedecked fireplaces (although one cocktail really has to go a long way). Restaurant-wise there is the obligatory gastro (two-star) L'Abeille, run by Philippe L'Abbé, and the Cantonese restaurant, Shang Palace, has one Michelin star. However, if I had to choose (and so far I have not been obliged to) I think I would prefer the Bauhinia, a less formal room, yet still splendidly grand with its coupole designed by Maurice Gras. The food is French-Asian fusion.

10, avenue d'Iéna · Paris 16ᵉ · Tel. +33 (0)1 53 67 19 98
www.shangri-la.com/paris/shangrila/

Billionaires'
hang-out.

Sunday in Paris

Where to shop on Sunday

With the exception of the Marais, a vibrant shopping and strolling hotspot, *commerçants* in most *quartiers* are completely deserted on Sunday. A good number of food shops are open until about midday and there are many morning markets, including Place des Fêtes in the 19th, Marchés Grenelle and Convention in the 15th, Bastille and Aligre* in the 12th, Les Enfants Rouges* in the 3rd and the famous organic market on boulevard Raspail* in the 6th. Check the city's website for times and addresses: www.paris.fr/english.

Coolfoodhunting

All the big food halls – Lafayette Gourmet, La Grande Épicerie de Paris*, Fauchon* – are closed on Sundays, so if you want to organize a little *diner* or *apéritif dinatoire* (so *chic*), you could pop over to Terroirs d'Avenir* on rue du Nil (meat, fish, vegetables, cheese) and shop like the chefs do. Da Rosa* in Saint-Germain is open for all delectable pork-based nibbles and *chez* Jacques Genin* you can pick up some chocolates, and a cake if you have managed to order beforehand. Thankfully, Pierre Hermé's* store on rue de Vaugirard is open until 5 pm, rue Bonaparte until 7 and his counter at the Publicis Drugstore on the Champs (133, avenue des Champs-Élysées, Paris 8ᵉ) until 10:30, a real lifesaver when the Sunday evening blues are too much to bear.

Finding a restaurant *en famille* on Sundays

Many smaller restaurants are closed on Sundays, but the brasseries are traditional places for lively family lunches and dinners. Those on boulevard Montparnasse, near the cinemas, are open all day for a quick plate of oysters, a chocolat chaud or a full-scale meal. My favourites are La Rotonde (105, boulevard Montparnasse, Paris 6ᵉ) and the eye-wateringly expensive

Le Dôme (108, boulevard du Montparnasse, 14ᵉ). Le Fooding's website has a very useful *'ouvert le dimanche'* filter for good, smaller restaurants open on Sundays: www.lefooding.com.

Breakfast and brunch

If you're out early around the Champ-de-Mars or les Tuileries, stop for breakfast in Carette* or Café Marly*. Drouant, a famous literary brasserie (it houses the Goncourt and Renaudot prizes), lays on a great value brunch in comfy surroundings (16–18, place Gaillon, Paris 2ᵉ). For the homesick, up near la place de Clichy, Le Bal Café's* brunch has porridge, kippers, bacon and eggs (6, impasse de la Défense, Paris 18ᵉ). For something more exotic you could try Liza's Lebanese brunches on 14, rue de la Banque, Paris 2ᵉ.

Also open on Sunday

It's worth heading to Villa 9 Trois (28, rue Colbert, 93100 Montreuil-sous-Bois) for a long and delicious Sunday lunch (it's closed in the evenings) in a pretty *terrasse* garden, where chef and famous author Stephane Reynaud has transformed a spacious *hôtel particulier* into a thriving restaurant. Special mentions for his rum Baba and foie gras. Other solid choices are: the Chinese Chez Ly (95, avenue Niel, Paris 17ᵉ) and Shan Gout (97, rue de Charenton, Paris 12ᵉ); the Vietnamese Paris Hanoi (74, rue de Charonne, Paris 11ᵉ) – be prepared to queue; the excellent family-friendly Italian Casa Bini (36, rue Grégoire de Tours, Paris 6ᵉ); the brasserie Flottes (2, rue Cambon, Paris 1ᵉʳ); and the elegant Montalembert (3, rue Montalembert, Paris 7ᵉ), right next to L'Atelier Saint-Germain de Joël Robuchon, where you can book the early sitting at 6:30 pm but must take your chances afterwards.

By the fire

The hotels L'Esprit Saint-Germain (22, rue Saint-Sulpice, Paris 6ᵉ) and Montalembert (see above) both have cosy fireside corners, while the patio and outdoor fireplace at L'Hôtel Jules and Jim (11, rue des Gravilliers, Paris 3ᵉ) is fantastic for a winter cocktail. Equally good for wine and cocktails around the hearth is the Compagnie des Vins Surnaturels (7, rue Lobineau, Paris 6ᵉ).

* See index page 202

Continued overleaf →

Sunday food and fun

Marché aux Puces de Saint-Ouen and Ma Cocotte

Take your time to discover the many different villages in this mini-town of antiques, *brocante* and art deco, and stop for lunch at Philippe Starck's new 250-seater canteen, Ma Cocotte (106, rue des Rosiers, 93400 Saint-Ouen), where *le Tout-Paris* flocks. Make sure you book.

Marché aux Puces de Montreuil and Chatomat or Mama Shelter

Much more of a bazaar than the chic and expensive Puces de Saint-Ouen, this sprawling market of second-hand clothes and white elephant oddities will have you rummaging more than oohing and aahing. Not far are Chatomat (6, rue Victor Letalle, Paris 20e), a delectable little gastro-bistro, and another Starck spot, Mama Shelter*, good for brunch with the kids or a cosy chocolat chaud.

Grand Palais and Mini Palais

After an exhibition at the Grand or Petit Palais head to the magnificent Mini Palais* dining room or its gorgeous stone terrace, one of the most beautiful in the capital (3, avenue Winston Churchill, Paris 8e). Open all day, but booking is essential. A great place for afternoon tea or a cocktail.

La Maison Rouge and Rose Bakery*

This huge disused factory was transformed in 2004 by private art collector Antoine de Gaudet into a dynamic home for private exhibitions, artistic experimentation and expression. Rose Carrarini has taken over the food, and three times a year the décor is changed and a pop-up café reflects the art being shown in the surrounding space. Ambitious and well worth a visit (10, boulevard de la Bastille, Paris 12e).

La Gaité Lyrique and Derrière

La Gaité Lyrique (3 bis, rue Papin, Paris 3e) is a digital arts and modern music centre opened in December 2010. It's a great spot for geeks and teens and only a short walk from the wonderful labyrinth of rooms that is Derrière (69, rue des Gravilliers, Paris 3e), a hipper than hip restaurant and salon de thé, full of quaint art and vintage bric-a-brac.

The Palais de Tokyo and Monsieur Bleu

The most spectacularly beautiful restaurant to open in Paris for many years was designed by interior architect Joseph Dirand. With a long *terrasse* overlooking the Seine, Monsieur Bleu (13, avenue du Président Wilson, Paris 16ᵉ) suddenly allows you to make a day out of a trip to the Eiffel Tower or to the contemporary art exhibitions at the Palais de Tokyo. There's all-day service, and highlights include an awesome Wagyu cheeseburger, oysters and impressive desserts.

Le Balzac and a steak at the Drugstore

A member of the Étoile cinema group, Le Balzac (1, rue Balzac, Paris 8ᵉ) has withstood the fierce competition from the international cinemas further down the Champs-Élysées and still programmes smaller budget indie films. After catching a movie here, grab a steak tartare from l'Aveyron at the Drugstore Steakhouse (133, avenue des Champs-Élysées, Paris 8ᵉ), open and serving all day.

... or Le Balzac and a cocktail at Le Marignan*

A discreet, small luxury hotel contrasting successfully with the glitzy palaces in the area. Behind the huge dark doors lies a little gem of interior design, signed by French wunderkind Pierre Yovanovitch, fast becoming famous for his crisp, masculine lines and use of luxurious materials. The *très* contemporary décor of the bar creates an elegant and laid-back atmosphere – the perfect place for a post-movie cocktail (12, rue de Marignan, 8ᵉ).

* See index page 202

NO

Don't forget to book

Turning up and hoping for the best
is not to be advised on Sundays
for anything other than a post-stroll
hot chocolate. Make sure you book
your concert, film, exhibition
and restaurant.

↑ Pâtisserie des Martyrs

8

Gourmet tours*

↑ Meert

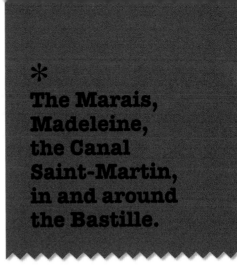

*

The Marais, Madeleine, the Canal Saint-Martin, in and around the Bastille.

Here are a few ideas for days when you have a good appetite, a carefree soul and enough time to take your time. The Marais, the Canal Saint-Martin and the Bastille all offer incredible variety, vitality and creativity in their choice of new places to eat. All it takes is one brave pioneer to open a bistro on an unassuming street. If it's good, the locals will keep coming back until someone lets the cat out of the bag to a critic or blogger and, *boom*, it's the new hottest thing in town. Once the newbie is established, others will try their luck nearby. Then, suddenly, it's become a foodie hotspot, an oasis of new places begging to be discovered. In other neighbourhoods, like the Place de la Madeleine, quality upscale destinations are a no-brainer. And you're sure to find your own treasures in this gastronomic paradise, just sharpen your senses and start walking.

The Marais

Rue de Bretagne in the north Marais is a truly authentic foodie hotspot and a good place to start a stroll around this beautiful part of Paris.

Market

The Marché des Enfants Rouges (see page 116) is a charming and historic slice of Parisian history – and the city's oldest covered market, restored in the '90s. Pick up something from the street food sellers' global offerings, then take a seat and watch the (rather hipster) world go by.

Marché des Enfants Rouges
Tuesday to Sunday
39, rue de Bretagne · Paris 3ᵉ

Pâtisserie

Further along is one of the latest concepts to get the food journalists and trend spotters buzzing: Popelini. Created in a couple of dozen flavours (like macarons) and presented in long rectangular slide-open boxes (like Nespresso), popelini are little bite-size choux, so light you hardly know you're eating them – honest! There's a fresh cream recipe *du jour* as well as standards like rose and raspberry or milk chocolate and passion fruit, and new flavours, such as Grand Marnier, are introduced all the time.

Popelini · 29, rue Debelleyme · Paris 3ᵉ · Tel. +33 (0)1 44 61 31 44 · popelini.com

Popelini →
↓ Poilâne

Tartines

On the rue de Bretagne, there are a lot of typical grocers, butchers, bakeries, as well as the *terrasses* of cool Café Charlot and Le Progrès, but a little further on you'll find the Cuisine de Bar de Poilâne, the restaurant address of the world-famous bakery. Here, the bread gets to show off as the base for a delicious range of tartines, next to a salad or a soup. Prettily designed, with white tableware by Le Petit Atelier de Paris, it's a fast, easy stop.

Cuisine de Bar de Poilâne · 38, rue Debelleyme · Paris 3ᵉ · Tel. +33 (0)1 44 61 83 39
www.cuisinedebar.com/en/index.php · www.poilane.com

Waffles and cookies

You'll need to walk all this off, most probably, so make your way through this impossibly *typique*, ancient *quartier* of Paris, perhaps stopping at the Café des Musées (see below) for a coffee (while imagining yourself in a 1920s film set) before a further sugar onslaught at Meert, the Parisian outpost of the celebrated Lilloise gaufres. The dainty, flat waffles filled with vanilla buttercream mixed with homemade icing (confectioners') sugar (how dedicated is that?) were a *péché mignon* of Charles de Gaulle. And try their more modern, adventurous versions with speculoos (spiced shortcrust biscuits), praline, cherry and pistachio flavours.

Meert · 16, rue Elzévir · Paris 3ᵉ · Tel. +33 (0)1 49 96 56 90 · www.en.meert.fr/

↑ Meert
Le Café des Musées →

Bistros

These two pillars of Parisian bistro culture are good-value stalwarts of traditional French food. Au Petit Fer à Cheval is owned by Xavier Denamur, fierce defender of real French food, so you will find no microwaved and parsley-topped impostors on your plates here. All the food is sourced with care and cooked on the premises. Similarly, at the Café des Musées, it's simple, hearty and tasty. Take your time.

Au Petit Fer à Cheval · 30, rue Vieille du Temple · Paris 4ᵉ
Tel. +33 (0)1 42 72 47 47 · www.cafeine.com
Café des Musées · 49, rue de Turenne · Paris 3ᵉ
Tel. +33 (0)1 42 72 96 17 · cafedesmusees.fr

Au Petit Fer à Cheval ↑

Madeleine

These addresses may seem a little clichéd, a little old-fashioned, too tailored to a tourist's idea of what French cuisine should be: all luxury, bows and cute boxes. But that said, they are perfect for those who are cash rich but time poor, looking for quick, edible Parisian spoils – and they are concentrated within a 200-metre (220-yard) radius.

Pâtisserie/delicatessen

Let's start at Fauchon – I usually do because, when I drive, as a serial valet parker I can leave them my car for an entire afternoon, even if all I'm picking up there is a croissant (shh!). Anyway, it's rarely *just* a croissant; I love the cakes here. The collections are gorgeous and ever changing. It was Fauchon's ex-pâtissier Christophe Adam who started the current craze for eclairs (and he has now opened his own eclair store) and who dared to mix them up, along with millefeuilles, in sweet and savoury versions. It will be interesting to see what the new pâtissier, Fabien Rouillard, brings to this historic address.

Fauchon · 24–26, place de la Madeleine · Paris 8e · Tel. +33 (0)1 70 39 38 00
www.fauchon.com/en/

Truffle shop and restaurant

Moving anti-clockwise around the place de la Madeleine, the next stop is at the Maison de la Truffe. The staff here are adorable and will take time to explain (in English if you so wish) the seasons, the different types, origins and ways of preserving and using the truffles they sell. You can either buy the real thing or select something from their excellent range – ravioli, confits, truffled brie – or even sit and try a few truffle dishes in the (rather formal) restaurant.

Maison de la Truffe · 19, place de la Madeleine · Paris 8ᵉ · Tel. +33 (0)1 42 65 53 22 maison-de-la-truffe.com

↑ Fauchon
Maison de la Truffe →

Wine store

Next, just round the corner, is the famous wine shop Lavinia. Spanning three floors, with over 6,000 different wines, it's perfect if you're looking for something in particular. You can also choose a bottle, have it opened and taste it at the bar with a bite to eat, or try one of the *grands crus* they offer by the glass.

Lavinia · 3–5, boulevard de la Madeleine · Paris 8ᵉ · Tel. +33 (0)1 42 97 20 20 www.lavinia.fr

↑ Lavinia
Ladurée →

Tea room and shop

Lastly, Ladurée. If only because the store is the original one, now renovated and extended to house the hundreds of spin-off products these sweet little macarons have generated in so few years. I'm old enough to miss the original boutique and salon de thé, with the creaky floors and, once, a cheeky little mouse after my chocolate macaron crumbs.

Ladurée · 16, rue Royale · Paris 8ᵉ · Tel. +33 (0)1 49 27 01 95 · www.laduree.com

Ladurée ↑

The Canal Saint-Martin

Despite the colour of the water being a bit off-puttingly murky, the Canal Saint-Martin allows a charming waterside stroll with lots of great food stops along the way. This is hipster central, and new places are popping up all the time, but these are the ones that I love most and, I believe, best define the Parisian food mood of the moment.

Grocery store/bistro

You could start your walk on the very, very cute rue Sainte-Marthe. Like the immediate area, it's still very rough and ready, but its tiny shop fronts are just crying out for more food pioneers to open them up, add a bit of Scandi retro design and attract the crowd hungry to taste the latest, well, everything. And, luckily for us, La Tête dans les Olives got there first. A tiny olde shoppe created by Sicilian olive oil lover Cedric Casanova. One side of the store holds cans and bottles of olive oil you can taste and learn about as if it were wine. Elsewhere, there are baskets of elephant garlic, dried basil and pink peppers, lotions and potions (irresistible packaging alert!) made from the best Sicilian tomatoes and lemons. The tiny space is transformed, by reservation only, into a table d'hôte, where chefs are invited to come and cook with whatever has arrived from Sicily that week.

La Tête dans les Olives · 2, rue Sainte-Marthe · Paris 10e
Tel. +33 (0)9 51 31 33 34 · www.latetedanslesolives.fr

Wine bistro

After taking a peek, or even a nap, inside the Hôpital Bichat's charming gardens, cross the canal and head towards Le Verre Volé. Since it opened in 2000, this place has become a true institution and *haut lieu* of natural and organic wines. The plates are masterpieces of Parisian foodie name-dropping, and range from quick snacks of charcuterie as alibis for opening a bottle from the hundreds around you (there's a supplement) to a full meal. Reservations are a must, but if you've missed out you could always walk a bit further and catch a little of Le Verre Volé's *philosophie* at their new Épicerie – serving some of the best sandwiches in Paris.

Le Verre Volé · 67, rue de Lancry · Paris 10ᵉ · Tel. +33 (0)1 48 03 17 34
L'Épicerie du Verre Volé · 54, rue de la Folie Méricourt · Paris 11ᵉ
Tel. +33 (0)1 48 05 36 53 · www.leverrevole.com

↑ La Tête dans les Olives
Le Verre Volé →

Restaurants

A little further down, on the other side of the canal, is the Hôtel du Nord, one of the best spots in Paris to give in to the cliché and people-watch on its *terrasse* for hours. It might be a shame to eat there, however, when Philou is just a few minutes' away. Philou is one of those places, along with restaurants Spring and Frenchie, that have been 'discovered' by *les anglo-saxons* in Paris – so why would I be indifferent? Don't expect, then, to hear only French spoken around you but the cuisine and wines are uncompromisingly French and hearty, especially during the game season.

Hôtel du Nord · 102, quai de Jemmapes · Paris 10ᵉ
Tel. +33 (0)1 40 40 78 78 · www.hoteldunord.org/english.html
Philou · 12, avenue Richerand · Paris 10ᵉ · Tel. +33 (0)1 42 38 00 13

Hôtel du Nord →
↓ Du Pain et des Idées

Bakery

Switching canal banks again, and moving south, la rue Yves Toudic has recently become one of the most pleasant for fashion shopping. On the corner is the beautiful *boulangerie* Du Pain et des Idées, selling Paris's best sourdough and mind-bogglingly gourmand tartes and viennoiseries. My very favourite thing here is, however, the sacristain – puff pastry filled with crème pâtissière. The unbelievably light pastry floats away in your mouth, leaving only caramelized sugar from the base to crunch between your teeth.

Du Pain et des Idées · 34, rue Yves Toudic · Paris 10ᵉ
Tel. +33 (0)1 42 40 44 52 · www.dupainetdesidees.com

... ssein de salades aux herbes
...dare de St Jacques et huîtres claires
Ballotine de poulet au lard et basilic
Risotto à la truffe noire (+10)

Pavé de Cabillaud, épinards tièdes aux couteaux
Coquilles St Jacques rôties, purée de céleri rave (+4)
Joue de Boeuf, blettes fondantes
Poulet fermier rôti, grenailles et champignons
Carré de Porc rôti, endives
Rognon de Veau, petits légumes

Baba au rhum
Gelée de litchi, crème de thé
Fondue au chocolat, fruits et choux
Pomme rôtie, glace caramel
Parfait au Café

Alsace, Riesli...
Vin de pays de l'A...
Mâcon-Chaint...

Chinon, Les F...
Fleurie, Chi...
Côtes-du-Rhône,
Vin de Pays de l'...
Morgon. Man...
Alsace, Pinot ...
Bandol, Do...
Vacqueyras, ...
Saint Emilion ...
Vin de Pays de l'...
Beaumes de Ve...
MORGON, MARC...

Philou ↑

Around the Bastille

A vibrant yet laid-back *quartier* of Paris, where you can easily while away the day admiring and tasting the food and getting a feel for how trendy Parisians live these days.

1 Market

This area has fast attracted a concentration of good restaurants around the excellent Marché d'Aligre and leafy place Trousseau, filled with *pétanque* players and a playground for kids. Built in 1779, situated behind the Bastille, an area which was the incubator of many uprisings, the market still has a popular, if no longer rebellious, feel about it, and people from all ethnicities come here to shop, drink and eat. Bric-a-brac, fabrics and old bookstalls mingle amongst the fruit and vegetables in the streets around the covered market.

From Tuesday to Sunday · Place d'Aligre · Paris 12ᵉ

Restaurants

Just round the corner, in rue de Cotte, is La Gazzetta, where one of Paris's trailblazing chefs, Peter Nilsson, turns out his singular, inspired dishes for a handful of euros at lunchtime and gets more gastro in the evenings. A little further on, Peter's ex-second, Giovanni Passerini, opened Rino, to further critical acclaim. On the corner, the Costes empire has taken over the sprawling, picturesque brasserie Square Trousseau (its former chef, Philippe Damas, is now cooking at Philou) and it's the perfect spot to read the papers with an *apéro* after the market.

La Gazzetta · 29, rue de Cotte · Paris 12ᵉ · Tel. +33 (0)1 43 47 47 05
lagazzetta.fr/wordpress/
Rino · 46, rue Trousseau · Paris 11ᵉ · Tel. +33 (0)1 48 06 95 85
www.rino-restaurant.com
Square Trousseau · 1, rue Antoine Vollon · Paris 12ᵉ
Tel. +33 (0)1 43 43 06 00 · www.squaretrousseau.com

← Square Trousseau
La Gazzetta ↓

Bakery

A few doors down is Blé Sucré, the bakery–pâtisserie *chérie du coin*.
There are two or three tables to linger at outside and savour your
purchases right away, and an incredibly good selection of bread,
sandwiches and cakes inside.

**Blé Sucré · 7, rue Antoine Vollon · Paris 12ᵉ · Tel. +33 (0)1 43 40 77 73
blesucre.fr**

Blé Sucré →
↓ Le Chocolat Alain Ducasse

Chocolate factory and store

Alain Ducasse has been working with chocolatier Nicolas Berger for
over ten years, supplying the Ducasse empire's hotels and restaurants
with their bespoke chocolates. For this new, original Parisian project – a
magical bean to bar chocolate factory and store – the two men sourced and
adapted (beautiful) vintage machines to roast and conch on site, and it's
all on show – scents, sights and sounds. They perfected the manufacturing
process as they went along, creating a range of stunning chocolate with the
finest beans such as Venezuelan Chuao or Peruvian Porcelana.

**40, rue de la Roquette · Paris 11ᵉ · Tel. +33 (0)1 48 05 82 86
www.lechocolat-alainducasse.com**

VIENNOISERIES

CROISSANT	0,90€
CHOCOLATINE	1,00€
PAIN AUX RAISINS	1,10€
ROULÉ AUX AMANDES	1,30€
CHAUSSONS POMMES	1,30€
BRIOCHE BOULE	1,00€
TARTE CARAMEL	1,10€
TARTE FRAMBOISES	1,10€
PAILLE D'ARGENT	1,50€
PAIN CHOCOLAT BLANC	1,10€
VIENNOISE	0,90€
...CHET DE MADELEINES	

Blé Sucré ↑

Paris food lover's roadmap

Rue Daguerre

A great place to head to on Sundays, when the streets around
are closed to traffic and the *quartier* gets even more animated
than usual. Names to look out for are bistros Le Jeu de Quilles
(45, rue Boulard) and Le Bis* (16, rue des Plantes), and for food
shopping on the rue Daguerre: Cave des Papilles (35) for natural
wine pilgrims; O Sole Mio (44), an Italian deli with freshly made
dishes and a great range of pasta; cheese shop Vacroux et Fils (5);
and L'Autre Thé (32) for fine teas.

Rue de Belleville

Even more *populaire* is rue de Belleville. From metro Belleville
up to rue des Pyrénées, it's an Asian food paradise, with a horde
of Vietnamese, Chinese and Thai restaurants, takeaways and
food shops (and Le Baratin* holding its own, tucked in at 3, rue
Jouye Rouve). The stretch I love particularly is between metros
Jourdain and Pyrénées, overlooked by the spires of Église Saint-
Jean Baptiste. There's an excellent tripe seller at number 130,
just along from the cheese shop Fromagerie Beaufils at number
118. Opposite the church, the bakery Au 140, at number 140, has
excellent bread, tarts and simple pastries like rochers, tuiles and
buttery palmiers.

Rue des Martyrs

Rue des Martyrs has recently become even more of a cake
lover's paradise. Rose Bakery* (46) was the pioneer of carrot
cakes and scones when the area was nowhere near as hip as it is
now. Newcomers Pâtisserie des Martyrs* (22), by the wonderful,
design-crazy Sébastien Gaudard, and mini choux à la crème
franchise Popelini* (44) join Arnaud Delmontel's excellent, if more
classic, *boulangerie–pâtisserie* at number 39. If you're craving
something savoury to put in a Delmontel baguette, Terra Corsa,
at number 42, has one of the best selections of Corsican cheeses,
wines and hams in Paris.

Boulevard Saint-Germain

Perhaps the best *épicier* in Paris is Da Rosa*, at 62, rue de Seine. So much sexier than its often aspic-obsessed French counterparts (it recently had a makeover by designer Jacques Garcia), it is a temple of hams and a specialist of Greek, Portuguese, Basque, Spanish and Italian fine foods. At number 81, Grom sells the only ice cream in Paris that has managed to rival Berthillon's* popularity. Across the boulevard Saint-Germain, Poilâne* at 8, rue du Cherche-midi; Hermé* at 72, rue Bonaparte; Gérard Mulot at 76, rue de Seine; and Jean-Charles Rochoux's chocolates at 16, rue d'Assas are all nestled amongst the fashion and design boutiques and are well worth stepping into.

Rue du Nil

This unassuming little street has suddenly become *the* hub of foodie hype. Not only are Gregory Marchand's three Frenchie* establishments – restaurant, wine bar and takeaway – situated here, at numbers 5–6, but also his (and many other excellent chefs') most trusted suppliers, Alexandre Drouard and Samuel Nahon, have opened Terroirs d'Avenir* at number 7, selling highest-quality restaurant *couture* poultry, fish, beef, cheeses, fruits and vegetables. If you *really* want to cook like a chef, start here!

* See index page 202

NO

Rue de Buci

Sadly, the village
feel has all but gone
from Saint-Germain-des-Prés,
and the food on offer
around rue de Buci
now reflects
the tourist onslaught.

Bonjour Paris

A rich, lively and beautifully written site with a wealth of info on all aspects of visiting, living in and enjoying Paris.

www.bonjourparis.com

Le Fooding

For festive hipsters and novelty obsessives. This French-language site includes brief descriptions of each address in English, and is worth checking out because their restaurant search engine is the most efficient I've seen anywhere.

www.lefooding.com/guide-restaurant-paris-France

French Food Fool

Der Spiegel reporter Ullrich Fichtner's food blog. With recipes, reviews and lots of cheese history. Lively, luscious and informed. A lovely insider's look at Paris.

frenchfoodfool.com

David Lebovitz

The famous pastry chef, author and blogger's website is a joy to behold and read, for gourmets everywhere. Great writing and wry insight into his 'sweet' life in Paris.

www.davidlebovitz.com

Alexander Lobrano: Hungry for Paris

Alec Lobrano is a superlative writer and connoisseur of French food and wine. You can follow his recommendations and beautiful writing here on his site and in his pieces for publications all over the world.

alexanderlobrano.com

Lost in Cheeseland

Lindsey Tramuta fell in love with a Frenchman and moved to Paris six years ago. Now she writes and muses about her Parisian life – and food – both on this lovely blog and for various international publications.

www.lostincheeseland.com

Mad about Paris

Neither a travel guide, nor a city blog: both of these and so much more. Ullrich Fichtner and Martina Meister's website includes a lot of food but winds it deliciously through Paris's culture and history.

madaboutparis.com

Adrian Moore

Concierge at the Mandarin Oriental, Adrian has first-hand knowledge of what is hot and new in Paris. His blog is punchy and assertive, his taste excellent.

www.adrianmoore.blogspot.fr

Paris

The Ville de Paris website is excellent and practical. Great for information on small local markets and *fêtes*.

www.paris.fr/english

Paris by Mouth

Paris by Mouth is a collective of Parisian food writers, and their website is a fantastic mine of information. They also organise wonderful gourmet walking and market tours in the Marais, Marché d'Aligre and Saint-Germain.

parisbymouth.com

The Paris Kitchen

Wendy Lyn is the queen of Parisian chef groupies and gets all the gourmet scoops and info. Her walks and classes are deliciously designed around some of the most famous cult cakes and desserts in the capital. A special mention for the riz au lait session at L'Ami Louis.

thepariskitchen.com

Cookery and wine classes, and guided tours

Context Walking Seminars

This excellent worldwide walking seminar company organizes a great chocolate walk in Saint-Germain-des-Prés, explaining in detail how chocolate and many other famous cakes and desserts are made.

Tel. +33 (0)9 75 18 04 15 / from abroad +1 215 609 4471
www.contexttravel.com/city/paris/walking-tour-details/chocolate-walk

Cook'n with Class

A very extensive range of classes in Paris and also day trips to the Champagne region to discover its secrets. The market cooking class takes you shopping and then back to the kitchen to learn how to cook your ingredients.

21, rue Custine · Paris 18ᵉ · Tel. +33 (0)1 42 57 22 84
www.cooknwithclass.com

La Cuisine Paris

Perfect for monomaniacs and those requiring intensive, technical know-how. You'll come away an expert on macarons, baguettes, chicken or cheese. They also organise excellent three-hour foodie tours.

80, quai de l'Hôtel de Ville · Paris 4ᵉ · Tel. +33 (0)1 40 51 78 18
lacuisineparis.com

École Ferrandi

Beginners can become professional cooks and pâtissiers during a year's training, which includes an apprenticeship in a pro kitchen. There are also classes in English during June and July for experienced cooks.

28, rue de l'abbé Grégoire · Paris 6ᵉ · www.ferrandi-paris.fr/en

The French Way

Another food tour team based in Paris and in the south of France. Marion and Celia dub themselves 'professional hedonists', and in Paris will take you on gourmet tours as well as ones themed around wine and art in Montmartre and through the Bastille market.

Tel. +33 (0)6 27 35 13 75 · www.thefrenchway.fr

Invisible Paris

Non food, but lovely suggested walking tours through lesser-known streets and *quartiers* of Paris.

parisisinvisible.blogspot.fr

O Château

This lively and unpretentious wine bar and restaurant has an impressive vaulted stone cellar where they hold wine tastings and wine pairing dinners. The sommeliers are all fully bilingual and the selection of wines eclectic.

**68, rue Jean-Jacques Rousseau · Paris 1ᵉʳ · Tel. +33 (0)1 44 73 97 80
www.o-chateau.com**

On Rue Tatin

Famous author and cook Susan Loomis offers classes in Paris and in her lovely fifteenth-century Normandy kitchen. Lots of time spent learning and even more spent enjoying and tasting what you've cooked.

www.onruetatin.com

Paris Hanoi Laboratoire

A story of three brothers who started with a Vietnamese sandwich stall that grew into two restaurants. In 2011 they began giving classes in a converted factory. Now, the Paris Hanoi is the place to learn how to handle a wok and put Vietnamese flavours together. Classes are small, always with plenty of time to taste as you go, and they can accommodate English speakers.

**9, rue Mont-Louis · Paris 11ᵉ · Tel. +33 (0)7 60 54 08 48
www.parishanoi.fr/cours-de-cuisine**

Promenades Gourmandes

Paule Caillat and Aude Barbera are two true Parisiennes. This small but extremely warm, welcoming and professional outfit can take you on a gourmet tour, give you a lesson after a visit to the market or train you as a professional pâtissier.

Tel. +33 (0)1 48 04 56 84 · www.promenadesgourmandes.com

Patricia Wells

The queen of French cooking and writing gives regular classes in Paris and Provence, following her principles of simplicity, intense flavours and culinary excellence. Again, great fun while you're learning and an even better time when you sit down to eat and taste the wines Patricia loves and shares.

www.patriciawells.com/cooking

↑ Jacques Genin

Glossary of select French terms

apéro: short for *apéritif*, pre-dinner drinks and nibbles

arrondissement: an administrative district of certain large French cities; Paris is divided into 20 arrondissements, arranged in a clockwise spiral from the 1st (1ᵉʳ) in the centre to the 20th (20ᵉ) on the eastern edge of the city

BCBG/bon chic bon genre: preppy, subdued, innate French chic and behaviour

bien dans ses baskets: to feel good about oneself

bis: twice

bof: slang for 'I don't care', 'whatevs'

bouchée: a mouthful, or a small bite-sized appetizer

boucherie: sells predominantly beef products and some pork, game and poultry

bouchon: cork in a bottle, a traffic jam or a restaurant serving traditional Lyonnais dishes

boulangerie: bakery

brocante: car boot, bric-a-brac sale

bûche (de Noël): Yule log

cake de voyage: a dry pound cake, good for slicing on the move

canette au sang: ancient method of cooking duck in its own blood. Extracted using a special duck press

charcuterie: sells predominantly pork products

chérie du coin: local sweetheart

cocotte en fonte: cast iron casserole dish

commerçant: shopkeeper or stallholder

couteau d'office: small paring knife

en cuisine: in the kitchen

épicerie: grocer's, selling many canned and preserved goods, wines and soft drinks. Also usually has a limited selection of fruit and vegetables and a small refrigerated section with pre-wrapped cheeses and cooked meats. An **épicerie fine** will have a more luxurious choice, sometimes stocking brands such as Fauchon, Lenôtre or Albert Ménès.

formule: a set, all-inclusive or table d'hôte menu

franchouillard: crudely French. Clichéd, country-bumpkin French style

fromagerie: cheese shop

haut lieu: pinnacle, a place of the highest standing

hôtel particulier: detached upscale townhouse

lièvre à la royale: rich dish of hare cooked in blood and wine

à merveille: wonderfully, to perfection

marché du jour: daily market produce

mirepoix: finely chopped vegetables, forming base of sauces and stocks

moindre des politesses: the most basic level of politeness one could expect

Monop': pet name for Monoprix, a chain of supermarkets

moule à manqué: round sandwich/pound cake tin

oeufs meurette: Burgundy dish of eggs cooked in an onion and red wine sauce

onglet aux oignons: skirt/hanger steak with onions

péché mignon: special treat, a weakness for something naughty but nice

petite dînette: light dinner or supper

pains de mie: sliced sandwich loaves

plat à gratin: gratin dish

populaire: popular, of the people

quartier: neighbourhood, quarter

repas gastronomique: gourmet formal meal

réveillon: Christmas or New Year's Eve

sablé: shortbread or shortcrust pastry

en salle: front of house

tartine: a slice of bread, toasted or not, spread with butter or used as a base for an open sandwich

(en) terrasse: (on the) terrace – or paved or planted area – outside a café or restaurant with small tables and chairs for customers to enjoy alfresco dining

tout court: in short, simply, 'full stop'

traiteur: ranges from full-blown caterer to small grocer's shop, where they sell ready-cooked and prepared dishes and other items to take away

une valeur sûre: a sure bet, surefire

vendeur: salesman, seller, shop assistant

verrine: small bowl, cup, or glass – literally a small *verre* – highly popular for serving individual layered dishes

viennoiseries: croissants, pains au chocolat, brioches – sweet bread products which aren't classed as pâtisseries

General Index

Numbers in square brackets refer to the arrondissement(s) in Paris.
Italicised page numbers refer to pages containing an image only of the establishment.

Restaurants:

brasseries, bistros, wine bars, cafés

Markets

Kitchen- and tableware

Foodie blogs and websites

Cookery and wine classes, and guided tours

Index of Menus and Recipes

Le Marignan ↑

↑ 6 Paul Bert

Acknowledgements

Merci...

To the Flammarion dream team:
Gisou Bavoillot, Kate Mascaro,
Isabelle Ducat, Flavie Gaidon, Helen Adedotun,
Ellie Corbett and photographer
Christian Sarramon for their patience, passion
and professionalism throughout this adventure.

To my friends and fellow cake
obsessives Emma Beddington and Mark Diacono,
for the reality checks and on-tap encouragement.

To the restaurant critics who have shared tables
with me over the years and inspired my writing
(and my eating): Alexandre Cammas, François Simon,
Jay Rayner and Marina O'Loughlin.

And to Catherine Roig for her
invaluable support and energy.

I hope that there will be no changes to the practical details in this book between going to print and publication. They are hard to avoid completely and I apologise if some have slipped in. As for my future favourites, visit my website and I'll blog about them as they open (see p. 208)!

Editorial Director:
Ghislaine Bavoillot

Design:
Isabelle Ducat

Copyediting:
Nicole Foster

Typesetting:
Thierry Renard and
Gravemaker+Scott

Proofreading:
Helen Downey

Colour separation:
Reproscan

Printed in Slovakia
by TBB, a.s.

Simultaneously published
in French as
Gourmande : Carnet parisien
© Flammarion, S.A., Paris, 2013

English-language edition
© Flammarion, S.A., Paris, 2013

87, quai Panhard et Levassor
75647 Paris Cedex 13

editions.flammarion.com

13 14 15   3 2 1

ISBN: 978-2-08-020156-0
Dépôt légal: 09/2013

Irish food writer **Trish Deseine** has lived in Paris for almost thirty years. Her first recipe book was released in 2001, and she has since published over twenty-five cookery titles in French, becoming one of France's most celebrated cookbook authors, and has sold more than one million books worldwide.

Thanks to her unpretentious approach to food, her first book *Petits plats entre amis (Cooking with Friends)* was awarded the Ladurée and SEB prizes, and her second, *Je veux du chocolat! (I Want Chocolate!)*, published in 2002, won a Gourmand World Cookbook Award and became a bestseller in France and internationally. These were soon followed by other successful titles, including *Ma petite robe noire et autres recettes* (2006) and, more recently, *Grande Table, Petite Cuisine*, for which she received a Gourmand Award for the best book of simple recipes, in 2013.

Trish has also hosted several cooking shows on television, broadcast by RTE in Ireland and BBC Lifestyle around the world, including a series dedicated to her passion for Paris, *Trish's Paris Kitchen*. She is a regular recipe contributor to *Elle France* and *The Irish Times*, and in 2010 *Vogue Paris* named her as one of the forty women of the decade.

Find Trish online:
www.trishdeseine.com